# BETTER
## THAN NEW

# BETTER
## THAN NEW

Lessons I've Learned from Saving Old Homes

(AND HOW THEY SAVED ME)

## NICOLE CURTIS

ARTISAN

NEW YORK

Library of Congress Cataloging-in-Publication Data

Names: Curtis, Nicole, 1976– author.

Title: Better than new / Nicole Curtis.

Description: New York : Artisan, 2016.

Identifiers: LCCN 2016029700 | ISBN 9781579656676 (hardback) | ISBN 9781579657932
  (signed edition)

Subjects: LCSH: Curtis, Nicole, 1976– | Television personalities—United
  States—Biography. | Contractors—United States—Biography. | Rehab addict
  (Television program)

Classification: LCC PN1992.4.C875 A3 2016 | DDC 791.4502/33092 [B] —dc23 LC record
  available at https://lccn.loc.gov/2016029700

Design by Laura Palese

Artisan books are available at special discounts when purchased in bulk for premiums and
sales promotions as well as for fund-raising or educational use. Special editions or book
excerpts also can be created to specification. For details, contact the Special Sales Director
at the address below, or send an e-mail to specialmarkets@workman.com.

Published by Artisan
A division of Workman Publishing Co., Inc.
225 Varick Street
New York, NY 10014-4381
artisanbooks.com

Artisan is a registered trademark of Workman Publishing Co., Inc.

Published simultaneously in Canada by Thomas Allen & Son, Limited

Printed in the United States of America
First printing, September 2016

10 9 8 7 6 5 4 3 2 1

This is a work of nonfiction. However, the names and identifying characteristics of some
persons have been changed to protect their privacy, and dialogue has been reconstructed
to the best of the author's recollection.

*In memory of my Gram*

*And to my babies—*
*nothing matters more than you*

# CONTENTS

# BETTER THAN NEW

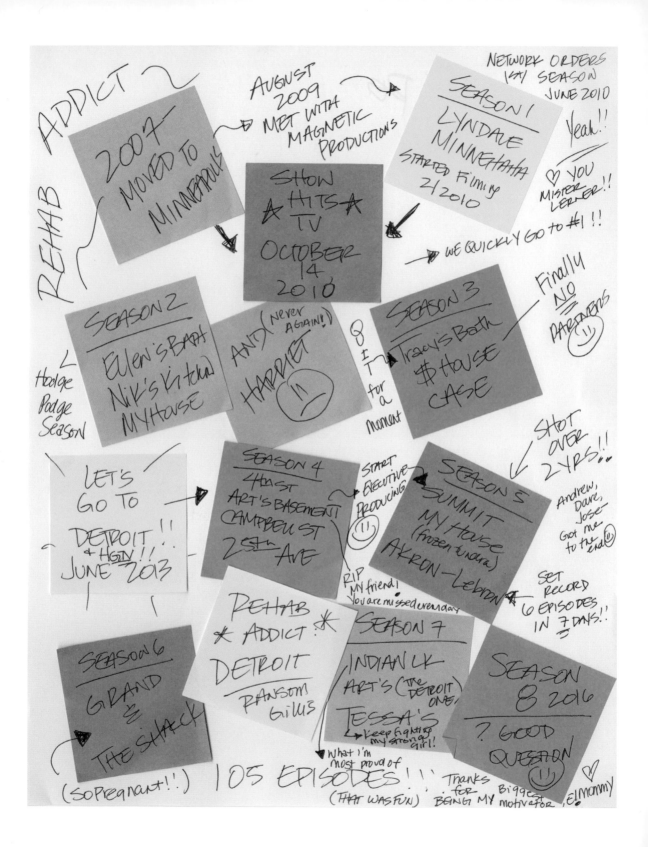

# PREFACE

Hi. I'm Nicole Curtis, and I'm addicted to rehab
(well, home rehab).

R*ehab Addict* is the name of my HGTV show, but it could just as easily be the title of my life. Ever since I can remember, I've fixed things. I was brought up in a family where that's just how it was. And every moment seemed to yield a lesson to learn. I heard "money doesn't grow on trees," "never judge a book by its cover," or my Gramps's favorite, "Do you work for Edison?" more often than I can count. These are lessons I carry with me to this day.

Throughout my childhood, I couldn't wait to have a home of my own, and at eighteen, I bought my first house. It seems like I've always been rehabbing a house. But as much as I put into my houses, as much as I believe they save neighborhoods and change people's lives, make no mistake—I get

Always the tomboy, only on holidays did I look picture-perfect.

something in return. The houses teach me valuable lessons. More than once, a dilapidated house that I've restored has actually helped save me, and given me a path to restoring the structure of my life. I'm here as proof: You can do a lot worse than listen to the lessons an old house can teach you.

As I've built my real estate and renovation career, I've come to associate particular lessons with a given house. The glorious Minnehaha mansion in southwest Minneapolis taught me that sometimes in order to move ahead, you have to be willing to let something go. That lesson keeps on ringing true. It has made me tackle

With my grandparents in 1979.

houses that others wouldn't touch, and that's led to a lot of success, both on and off my TV show. Whenever I think about the Dollar house in the Central neighborhood in Minneapolis, I remember that I need to be able to back up my words with action. For someone who is not afraid to speak her mind, that lesson is a good reality check. And even my first house, a feeble structure in Tampa, drove home the universally useful point that every mistake is knowledge waiting to happen.

I've renovated so many old houses that after a while, the lessons piled up and started to seem like a guidebook to a well-lived life. I realized that every new one was another page in the road map out of troubled times—not just for me, but for anyone. I write about these lessons in my social media posts and talk to friends and family about them, and now I'm collecting them in a book to pass on what I've learned.

LAKE ORION GIRLS
SOFTBALL LEAGUE 1987     87

"You're such a nice young man,"
I would hear so often.

* * *

I know it all started with my upbringing. I was born and raised in a small town called Lake Orion, right outside Detroit, Michigan. My parents taught me to work hard, be smart, and hang tough. My incredible grandparents, too, were part of my education. Children of the Depression, they knew what it was to have nothing and made sure each of us kids knew what it meant to work for a living. In fact, returning to my hometown to rehab their Indian Lake Road house brought me back to one of the most important lessons I learned from them: to live life on your own terms. My life might not seem "normal" to some, but what I've come to learn is that there is no "normal." I think that's been the most valuable lesson. You will never succeed in life judging yourself by someone else's standards.

I've been described as having a strong personality, which I take to mean I'm a woman who speaks her mind and stands her ground. Other people may have an issue with that, but I get into trouble anytime I lose touch with that woman. The houses I renovate—and their lessons—inevitably bring that part of me back, front and center.

I've always loved taking on challenges—what other people call "problems" and "roadblocks." It's a big part of what makes my business profitable and has led to my reputation as a savvy entrepreneur. Sure, on any given day you may lose more than you win. I'll be the first to admit that adversity isn't always fun. You have to be ready to fall and get right back up. But that's always easier if you're doing something you believe in, and when you know you can take away lessons from the experience. For instance, I didn't particularly want to rebuild a severely fire-damaged house on Campbell Street in Detroit, but doing so taught me that determination can be a tool, one that can transform a pile of ashes into a special home. That type of lesson is key to improving as a professional and as a person. I know it's how I get better at everything in life.

As I began to write this book, I realized I wanted to include more than just "lessons." A lot goes on behind the scenes of my show, and over the course of any long and involved historic home renovation. Sometimes I find myself in totally unexpected and surprising situations. I've swung a hammer next to LeBron James; Lenny Kravitz told me I was a badass; and Sia said she loved my show, not knowing that her song "Breathe Me" got me

My teens.

through more than one difficult moment. I'm always caught off guard by the fact that this little idea I had—to save houses that no one cared about—is celebrated by so many people worldwide. More often, I enjoy heart-tugging moments that seem to come out of the blue. I've been surprised on my set by fans who just showed up and brought me to tears with their inspiring stories. When someone says, "You've changed my life," I'm humbled, and I realize that all the "bad" I experience has purpose even if it takes me years to understand it. So much happens

My son Ethan through the years.

that the camera doesn't catch, and I wanted to share all that as well. There is simply a lot more to what I do than fixing up old houses.

A great friend once told me, "Nicole, if you understand business and people, you can do anything you want." I look at everything in life like I'm building a house. Whether it's helping others or working on my own personal issues, if you don't start with a solid foundation, it will all fall apart.

That's why, regardless of the difficulties and how successful I might be at overcoming them, I'm always looking to learn. I've gotten a graduate education from the joys and challenges in life. No degree out there will give you the skill sets required to go through life without making some mistakes. Believe me, I would have done anything to be handed a guidebook on the easy way to raise a teenager, manage businesses, age gracefully, and even prepare for the unexpected—things that have occurred in my life that I never could have imagined. But instead, you learn as you go. And if you take the lessons to heart, it helps you down the road.

When I started writing this book, a friend asked me a simple question: "What do you want readers to get out of it?" I paused for a long time before I replied, because there were a lot of answers to that question. I told him, "I want anyone who turns past the first page to understand that they can do it, whatever 'it' is." I've witnessed friends fight cancer, even when it was terminal, pushing back against overwhelming odds, never quitting, and the truth is, would anyone ever blame someone for wanting to give up that fight? But we find strength where we didn't know we had it, and this can make such a difference in our attitude and in our quality of life. Drawing inspiration from others has empowered me, and I hope that my words will do the same for you.

There's something else as well. As much as I want this book to teach readers, so that they can avoid making some of the same mistakes I've already made, I also want it to motivate my readers to tackle whatever constitutes their "old houses." The experiences I've had renovating old houses have helped me navigate being a woman in a traditionally male profession, given me the courage to build several businesses all by myself, and driven me to get back up and succeed after I lost everything and had to rebuild from scratch. So here are the best lessons I can give you, and hopefully you'll walk away with this one idea after you turn the last page: Passion and perseverance are the keys to success in whatever you choose to take on. I'm not the smartest person, I'm not the strongest person, and for years I didn't have two nickels to rub together, as my Gram would say, but if I can get through all the unexpected things (some good, some bad) that have popped up in my life—burned-out houses, rescue dogs, roller-coaster finances, tough business negotiations, and ugly people—you, my friend, can get through anything.

*FIRST RULE WHEN BUYING AN OLD HOUSE... FIRST DO NO HARM* :)

## Chapter I

# MISTAKES ARE KNOWLEDGE WAITING TO HAPPEN

### TAMPA HOUSE

**M**y parents didn't exactly jump for joy when I decided to dive head-first into adulthood by moving south with my boyfriend right after my high school graduation. They would have much preferred I go away to college. What parent wouldn't? I look back and think, Oh my gosh, I would have locked my daughter in the basement! They were worried, but they also knew me. Even at that age, I was headstrong. Once I decided to do something, I was going to do it. I was never the happy-go-lucky child. I was a bit of an overachiever bookworm, to say the least. Ever the leader, as student council president (later impeached—don't ask), I chose to spend spring break painting the ugly girls' bathroom of our high school with my friend

Cara and me in our student council uniforms (left). I looked like I could've been on the
Swiss Miss cocoa box in my IHOP days (right).

Cara Cowser. And I was obsessed with finding the keys to success in life
as soon as humanly possible. My parents' generation was taught that you
stayed in a good job, raised your kids, retired, and collected your pension.
The closer I got to graduating high school, the more I knew I had to follow a
different path. Telling me no just meant I would be all the more determined.
And I wasn't far from turning eighteen. The challenge you face with raising your children to always question everything is that sooner or later that
"everything" includes your opinion as a parent.

So my boyfriend, Steve, and I moved south. Our first stop was Atlanta,
and we soon realized why it is called "Hotlanta." Within five minutes, I
regretted that decision—it rained every day, with hot temps and humidity.

I had so much growing up to do, and unfortunately, I chose to spend
what should have been the best time of my life becoming what most people

dread: one half of a very difficult relationship. I had been catapulted into adulthood, by my own doing, and I had real bills—rent, gas, heat, food, and electricity—to pay. I didn't want to prove my parents right that I wasn't ready for this, so I just stuck it out. Job options were slim, so I got a job waitressing. And because I was still seventeen, and still a minor, I couldn't work where alcohol was served, so there I was looking like I fell off the Swiss Miss cocoa box at the IHOP in Woodstock, Georgia. I worked from 6 P.M. to 6 A.M., and on a good night I made fifty to sixty dollars in tips. Still, while my friends were living it up at college, I was working at the IHOP. Needless to say, as soon as I turned eighteen, I looked for a new job.

After a quick stint at an upscale Chinese restaurant, I took a friend's suggestion and applied at Hooters. I remember that the day I applied, I wore my favorite shredded MSU sweatshirt and cutoff jeans, and I had my hair in a braid. I was so excited, but Steve was not happy. I assured him it was fine. The "girls" at my Atlanta Hooters were like family. Steve warmed up to the idea after meeting them. They were students like me, teachers supplementing their income, and even moms—not wannabe strippers as most outsiders believed. I made great money there and just loved having older "sisters." As soon as I started getting comfortable in Atlanta, Steve was offered a job in Tampa. I contemplated staying behind on my own, but there I was on a Super Bowl Sunday packing up to go with him.

Steve and me (notice the infamous MSU sweatshirt) with Girlie, one of my first rescue dogs.

21

We settled in North Tampa. I was excited to focus on school, as we were right around the corner from the University of South Florida. We found a nice apartment—fifteen-hundred-dollars-a-month nice. Looking back, I think, Holy cow, that's as much as I would have paid each month had I bought a house. But this was long before my real estate days. For that moment, I felt like I had really made it, living in an upscale two-bedroom, two-bath luxury unit with all the amenities: dishwasher, granite counter-tops, plush carpeting, high-end tile, and a washer and dryer. The complex had a pool, a Jacuzzi, tropical landscaping—the works. But it was full of families and older professionals, so there wasn't much chance to hang out with people my own age. I spent any free time I had soaking up sun around the pool.

I've held on to my Hooters name tag for all these years; it reminds me how far I've come.

I would continue to get my Hooters education, as I referred to it. I'm sure a lot has changed in the past twenty years, but back in my Hooters days it was rare for a waitress or bar-tender position to become available. When I got to Tampa, there wasn't an opening, so I took a position at the Brandon store.

Soon after, a life-changing thing happened while I was getting my Florida driver's license. The clerk at the DMV, who just looked worn out, was having trouble with her reading glasses and kept adjusting them on her nose and then rubbing her eyes. I don't know what her problem was, but it turned out to be my good luck. She misread my date of birth, so instead of 1976, she put it down as 1971. Suddenly, with the stroke of a nearsighted clerk's pen, I was twenty-three. It was just one of those small mistakes in life that turned out to have big consequences.

With a valid ID, I could go out without Steve. Up to that point, if we wanted to go to a bar or a club, Steve had to slip the door guy or bartender a twenty to get me in. In other words, if I wanted to go out, I had to go out with Steve. Now I could go anywhere I wanted with just my girlfriends. It was yet another crack in the relationship. Maybe it just sped up the inevitable, but I remember this being monumental at the time.

Hooters, like the rest of Tampa, was money on parade. I had been raised in a completely different world. My family had always budgeted tightly and scrimped and saved. We were far from poor, but now I got to see how millionaires and multimillionaires lived. I thought, There's real money to be made in this world. This is the side of the fence I want to be on. It wasn't that I was fixated on money. I just did not want to struggle like my parents had. They had been hurt badly by the downsizing of the automotive industry. I wanted to avoid putting myself in a position like that.

For all of that, though, something else dawned on me, something that left me a little conflicted. I was raised to value a college education above all else. Where I came from, that was the ticket to a better life. But it hit me that if I went down the traditional road and paid to get a college diploma, what was going to change? I would probably go into debt for it. Then I was going to graduate and go to work for one of these guys at my tables? Making less money than I was making at Hooters? The reality of the situation just kind of drove me nuts. Looking back, I know now that there was a tough businesswoman in my head telling me, "Go your own direction."

In fact, that's how the entrepreneur in me looked at waitressing—like I had bought into my own private franchise within that Hooters. My section was *my* business. It was up to me how much I sold and how much I made. If I moved a lot of beer and chicken wings, the tab would come to a hundred dollars and I'd get twenty. The more tables I turned, the more money I made. I became a crazy waitressing machine. So much so, in fact, that Steve would find me waiting tables in my sleep. While other girls would hang out and socialize on a slow day, you would find me camped out by the front door waiting for people to come in and leading them to my tables.

I've always been someone who enjoys work. I babysat as soon as I could, and snagged my first real job—when I was twelve—working along with my best friend, Jaime, for a little over two dollars an hour plus all the strawberries we could eat, directing people who came to pick berries on a farm. (No wonder neither of us will go near a strawberry to this day.) My next job was at the car dealership where my aunt was the office man-

Me and Jaime—friends to this day.

ager. I remember sitting there dividing my hourly wage by sixty, calculating my earnings down to the minute. It was frustrating knowing that no matter how much energy I put in at the job, working for an hourly wage I could only make so much. Another friend brought me to work with her, where we did telemarketing for a carpet cleaning company. All I had to do was book appointments and I could earn bonuses. I loved it. I'm a pretty fast talker, and soon the rest of the employees gave me the look because I was outbooking everyone so much that the company changed the quotas. It was an early lesson in keeping your head down and your mouth shut, and to never discuss money.

That's exactly why waitressing was the perfect fit for me. All in all, Hooters turned out to be lucrative exactly because I looked at it like a business. And though I was more blatant than most, I wasn't alone. It wasn't lost on me that other waitresses were showing up for their shifts driving brand-new cherry-red Mustangs and convertible Corvettes and carrying around purses that cost as much as

Ethan in my Hooters shirt on Halloween.

I made in a week. You can gain knowledge from other people's mistakes as well as your own. And yes, the occasional waitress would be rocking a Chanel bag and shoes while she was two weeks past due on her rent, but for the most part, the Hooters staff was filled with smart, tough, independent women who knew how to run the game. Not exactly the stereotypical idea of a Hooters waitress. In fact, I'm still in contact with the girls I worked with, and they are some of the most seriously successful women I know. Of course, I take some heat from my teenage son, Ethan, who *loves* to just pop my Hooters factoid into conversations out of the blue. But there you go; my life's been lesson after lesson on how wrong conventional wisdom can be.

Business, for me, didn't stop at the doors of Hooters. I wanted to do more, a symptom of an eighteen-year-old's impatience and the drive to have it all now—not next month, not next year, but right now.

I come from a family of meticulous housekeepers. My Gram grew up in an orphanage. At as young as seven years old, she cleaned morning, noon, and night. As an adult, she took great pride in her house, and she always said, "Clean doesn't cost money; there's no excuse for your home to be dirty." I'm always amazed at the number of people who don't know how to clean their houses or mow their lawns. But as I found out in those first few years of adulthood, people love to pay people to do their dirty work. So I bought a ream of copier paper and some felt-tip markers, and drew up a bunch of flyers advertising my cleaning services: twenty-five dollars for a one-bed-room apartment, and thirty-five dollars for a two-bedroom. I taped them up all around the apartment complex and at some local stores, and the work came rolling in.

I had to keep in mind that not all people are good people with good intentions. There was the reality that you have to be careful when you're a young woman going into people's homes. You have to suspect that there's a jerk around every corner. I'd always leave a note for Steve with the client's

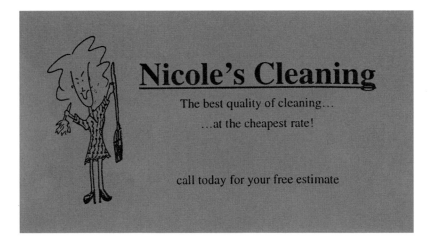

My first business card.

name and address. And I had no qualms about ditching a job. Always trust your gut. If I didn't feel safe, I left.

My clients were an eye-opener. You see the guy with a sixty-dollar haircut driving a Mercedes with a super-fashionable wife who probably thought I looked like a hot mess in my ratty T-shirt and shorts, and you think "success"—only to find that they were living in an apartment that was in an appalling state, with unopened mail, a clothes trail from living room to bedroom, a sink filled with dirty dishes, and three-day-old takeout containers cluttering the coffee table. It was a revelation that people could look so well put together and have such disorganized, messy homes. I was also amazed that people had brand-new TVs or expensive stereo systems and still lived in a rented apartment they were paying me to clean. They could keep the fancy stereo. I was all about owning a house. Cleaning someone else's was just a step along the path that led to my own front door.

The work became a compulsion. I would clean apartments as early as my customers would let me in, and then get to Hooters at ten thirty in the morning to work a double until after midnight, five days a week. I'd walk out with three hundred dollars. I'd come home each night, drag out the little wooden cash box I kept in the closet, and—before I even changed out of my Hooters outfit—count out the day's take. Add that to the cold hard cash I was getting paid to clean up other people's messes, and I was doing pretty well. Still, I felt defeated every month when I wrote the rent check. I wanted to be an adult.

Everything I did was to appear mature and prove my parents wrong. And getting rid of my Geo Tracker was part of that. The sad truth is that I didn't feel like much of a grown-up driving a white "jeep" with pink and teal accents. At eighteen, I thought image was everything, and that car didn't suit me. (What I wouldn't give now for a cute, dependable, sporty ride that cost me less than two hundred dollars a month!) As that wooden box got fuller, I started thinking I needed something that celebrated my success . . . something in the form of a gold BMW 328i convertible. (I know it's the last thing anyone would expect me to say now, but then . . .)

A BMW was exotic to me. I was also the child of a former autoworker, and being from Michigan, it was a sin to drive anything other than a car made by the big three American automakers. But I was trying to shed my past, and buying that car would lead to yet another valuable lesson.

The car was parked on a tiny used-car lot. I went in and got sold immediately. I remember the sales guy explaining Pirelli tires to me as "guaranteed to never go flat." (Oh, how I miss the naiveté that comes with being eighteen—I actually repeated this line to the tow-truck driver a few weeks later when I got a flat. He had a good laugh.) The car cost around thirteen thousand dollars, and I was referred to a local bank to get a loan. I filled out the credit application and was given a flat-out denial faster than a car depreciates after you drive it off the lot. I don't know what I was thinking. I didn't have any credit, and as a waitress making cash tips, my stated income was $3.25 an hour.

I drove home in defeat, in my hated Geo Tracker. Steve listened as I told him what had happened, tears of frustration welling up in my eyes.

"Hold on. Did you tell them how much you work at Hooters, how much you make in tips?" he asked me.

I stopped sniffling and looked at him. "No." That money fluctuated and was in cash, so I hadn't thought to put it on the credit application.

"Well, did you tell them about cleaning houses?"

"No."

He looked at me and said, "Give me the bank manager's number."

Steve, ever the charmer, with his charismatic personality, dark brown eyes, and perfect jet-black hair with just a touch of wave, could woo anyone, including me back then. I handed over the business card and he was on.

I could hear him carrying on with the bank manager. "How's your day going? Oh, come on now. You shouldn't be working so hard—you gotta have fun sometime." It might have sounded like a call leading to a date, but it was a pitch. A sales pitch. Steve got her laughing and engaged, which I learned was always your goal when trying to make a sale. He told her how hard I worked, and how most of what I made was paid in cash. He explained that my income would increase, as this was merely a first step for me. He pitched her like it was a foregone conclusion that I would get that loan—and of course I did. And listening to Steve describe my many great qualities, she must have thought she was lucky to have the privilege of giving it to me. I would have stumbled all over myself to give me a loan, too.

When he got off the phone, Steve explained, "It's not about the credit. You don't have credit. What you have is *you*. You need to promote you and everything you do."

It was all good in theory. So there I was, the proud owner of a gold BMW convertible . . . and a Geo Tracker. Steve got the bank to give me the loan, but he also agreed to give them the title to my Geo Tracker as collateral. I could hear my dad chastising me—collateral meant a lien on the title—but I was also damn proud of myself. I had been able to finance my dream car—I mean, kind of, not really, as my disappointed dad would explain later. And thinking back, I'm horrified by what a materialistic twit I was. However, down the road, when faced with the challenge of getting turned down for jobs because my résumé didn't list an applicable college degree, I would recall Steve's pitch to that loan manager and pick up the phone and sell the fact that I was much more valuable than what that piece of paper reflected. The truth is, no one can promote you better than you can. From that experience on,

My best friend, Chrissy, and me rocking the beach.

I knew it was up to me to show people that there was more to me than meets the eye if I wanted them to support me in whatever business I was doing.

I'm not going to lie; the car made me smile. But I still had my eye on the prize: a house of my own. Between my two jobs and Steve's commissions, we actually had a decent amount of money coming in, but we had no established credit. Getting a car financed was one thing, but having great credit to buy a house was something else. In 1995, the market was tight. It was a lot harder to qualify for a loan than it is today. We could afford a hefty mortgage payment, but we didn't have enough of a down payment for a bank to waive some of the other criteria. Interest rates were high, and there simply weren't the first-time-buyer opportunities there are now. Today, one of my dogs could get financing. But back then? An unmarried couple, with no real credit history? No way.

So I hunted for a less traditional way to get my hands on a house. Late one night Steve and I were watching a movie on TV when a Carleton Sheets infomercial came on during one of the breaks. If you don't know who Carleton Sheets is, you've never been desperate to own property without a down payment to get you in. Carleton Sheets was the original king of infomercials. The TV spot itself was exactly what you might envision: Sheets looking straight at the camera, talking right to you, earnest as hell, offering testimonials from people who had used his course to get rich, standing out-side their St. Petersburg Spanish Revival mansions. Some bald guy with a comb-over, a paunch, and a hot blond model wife letting you know that he never had to work again. Sheets seemed to be the height of trustworthiness. He looked like a country club golf pro—tall, blond, clean-cut, nicely dressed, with a great smile. He promised that you'd be able to buy a house, no money down, and make a huge profit from flipping it. Steve couldn't dial the 800 number fast enough. There was an operator standing by to take the order for our very own set of Carleton Sheets's *No Down Payment 12 Cassette Audio Home-Study Course.*

I made it through about three of those tapes. I never discovered the "secret" he was pitching, but I did learn about what is known as a "land contract." Also called a contract for deed, a land contract is simply an agreement for owner financing. The buyer usually agrees to a big bal-loon payment five to seven years into the loan and a higher overall interest rate in exchange for a very modest down payment. It also usually means paying way more than market value for a house. I didn't care about all that. I saw it as my ticket into the real estate market—and into our own home.

We pored over the real estate section of the *Tampa Bay Times* looking for land contract deals. Eventually, we found one that sounded perfect, for a house on the Gandy Peninsula. Back then the Gandy Peninsula was a deso-late, forgotten part of Tampa. It's a knob of land that juts out into Tampa Bay, exactly midway between Tampa and St. Pete, full of timeworn  neighbor-hoods clustered around MacDill Air Force Base. There was an air of sadness to the place. And the house, well, the best I can say is that it was *a house.*

The house on West Pearl Avenue was one of several homes that an older couple had bought to flip. They'd done the bare minimum—basically slapped some paint on the inside and laid the cheapest linoleum and carpeting they

The couple that gave me my first opportunity to own real estate (left). The West Pearl Avenue house (right).

could buy—and then sold the places on land contracts as their kids' inheritance. It was pretty ingenious, actually.

A note for fifty-eight thousand dollars (minus the three-thousand-dollar down payment) bought us a house that shook when you slammed the front door. It was a nine-hundred-square-foot, three-bedroom, one-bath midcentury. Not good midcentury, mind you, a Tampa, Florida, midcentury. Which translates to the cheapest construction you can find. I was used to northern homes. My parents built the house I grew up in and my dad was so proud of its "R value," which is basically the efficiency of the insulation. The higher the R value, the greater the insulating power. This house was a minus 20. There was no dishwasher or garbage disposal. The kitchen had simple metal cabinets, and everything was off-white, except for a couple of walls clad in faux wood paneling used in place of drywall.

As bad as the interior was, what surrounded the house was actually worse. At the side was a nondescript boxy apartment building, where

The green-and-black mosaic tile that I covered up!

people would dump their garbage along the fence when the dumpsters were full, providing a lovely smell. Our backyard hadn't been landscaped since Kennedy was president. The people in the houses around us were all seniors, many still working. They were nice, sweet people, but not exactly my contemporaries. There was a gas station on the corner and a crumbling Jai Alai across the street. In the middle of all that loveliness sat my new house.

But it was mine (well, Steve's and mine). Strange as it might seem, I was over the moon. You have to know this about me: I'm all about the good. I'm not really one for doing things slowly and carefully, weighing the pros and cons of any situation. Sure, this has gotten me into a jam or two. But if I were more cautious, I'd probably still be living in my parents' house, sleeping in my childhood bedroom, dreaming big dreams while staring up at my Lamborghini and Harvard posters.

Looking at this feeble house, I just saw potential. Whatever was wrong with it, I knew I could make it right. I focused on the fact that I had a house; I would deal with everything else. It didn't register for a second that I had paid twice what it was worth. I knew that paying more was the only way I was going to get into a house, so I made my peace with it. Our rent in the apartment had been $1,500, and our monthly house payment was $596.42. The way I saw it, whether we'd paid too much for the house or not, we were still saving money. Now I look back and think that Steve and I, with our fancy cars, didn't have a clue.

We didn't know to have the house inspected or appraised; the couple had assured us it was a great investment. I remember telling my uncle who was an electrician that the house had new wiring. He looked at me with hesitation and said, "All new wiring?" I said, "Yeah—they said it was new wiring." And I trust that it was—in 1957!

The first order of business was improvement. We started with the basics: new interior paint and some stick-down tile to cover up the mint-green-and-black mosaic in the bathroom. Yes, I said it. I covered up fantastic original tile. Even worse, I stuccoed the bathroom walls and added wallpaper. But come on—I also wore frosted lipstick back then! But beyond simple things like that, I found I was running up against a lack of knowledge. It was frustrating. I wanted to be able to do all the repairs myself, but as soon as I started on a project, I'd realize I was flying blind.

As much as I might have done wrong, I did a lot right. I threw myself into that house. It didn't bother me that in order to fit everything into my schedule, I often worked on the house in the middle of the night. Gardening meant weeding, digging beds, and planting hostas in the dark. I made that house into a little palace. It was the cutest house in the neighborhood. Maybe that particular bar was set low, but still.

Living in Tampa was really about me rethinking what I took to be gospel. Growing up, I had always assumed I would get married and settle down as soon as possible. I had been raised with the classic Motor City blue-collar ideal that meant you got a job and worked hard for somebody else. I had grown up thinking I would go to college, get a high-paying job, work for thirty years, and retire. But I was finding out that there are many different ways to survive in this world, and it doesn't have to mean working for somebody else from nine to five. I was also discovering that whatever I did, I could do it all myself. I just had to be willing to make mistakes, learn from them, and put those lessons into action.

Steve taking a crack at the new dining room.

Some of the most challenging mistakes were going to be the ones I made in home improvement. But those were also a way to gather really useful knowledge. For instance, it bothered me that my little house didn't have a dining room. Looking back, that seems like the least of its defects. But on the cusp of turning nineteen, I had a lot of ideas about being an "adult." One of them was that adults had dining rooms, and I was damn well going to have a dining room. Mind you, neither Steve nor I had a clue about what we were doing, but we did it. We got a saw and a sledgehammer and decided to add on to the house.

My new dining room with studs in place (left) and framed (right).

"Are you sure you want to do this?" Steve said.

"Of course I'm sure."

The way I figured it, we already had a foundation in the carport slab. The carport also gave us a roofline. All I had to do was cut an opening, put up some walls, and *bam*, I'd have my dining room. Yes, that was all I had to do.

And down went the wall. I blame it on Sade. Steve and I might not have had much in common, but we loved listening to smooth jazz. We always had Sade playing in the background, which somehow lent a Zen feeling to remodeling.

As anyone who has done even a small, basic room addition will tell you, I was being a little ambitious, to put it mildly. Cutting the opening from the living room through to the carport was the easy part. And when I say "cutting an opening," I mean haphazardly putting a huge hole in the wall, which was easy enough. Framing in the new room? Not so easy.

It wasn't until I had actually cut the hole that I realized framing in a room was not something I could snap my fingers to accomplish. We started trying to put studs in place, but it quickly became apparent that framing was beyond our pay grade. Especially when you consider I wanted glass patio doors.

We stood there, me sweating through my favorite Mean People Suck T-shirt, my dust mask hanging on my neck, and Steve as beat as I had ever seen him. We looked at each other and said, "We're in over our heads." Framing requires knowledge of basic homebuilding and carpentry and a mastery of construction math. This situation revealed the tiny flaw in my charge-ahead-and-you'll-figure-out-how-it's-done philosophy. We stapled three-millimeter clear plastic sheeting over the hole in the wall while I figured out how I was going to get the room framed.

I found the answer in the form of a handyman ad in the local *Pennysaver*. This guy was not a contractor, just a handyman paid by the hour. Then again, I wasn't looking for code-compliant work. At that point, I didn't even know what codes were. Much as I didn't want to, I hired the guy to frame and side the three exterior walls, and install the glass doors. In the end, I parted with some hard-earned Hooters cash, but I had a dining room. One with exposed studs and a concrete floor, yes, but a dining room. I even put up a couple of pictures on the studs. In keeping with my glass-half-full outlook, I looked at that room and saw a dining room straight out of a magazine. And I still remember the look of horror on Steve's very affluent mother's face when she visited. In that room she saw a disaster in the form of exposed studs and insulation and a painted concrete floor with a concrete step into the living room. As soon as she returned to Michigan after her visit, I received a large binder with "suggestions" for the house. I still have the book; it sits in my office. We've had our differences throughout the years, but I've held on to the book. If nothing else, to have a good laugh. I'm sure she never had a clue how much I'd take that all to heart.

On the other hand, when *my* parents came for a visit, they did what they could to throw some skills our way. By the end of their stay, we had painted vibrant colors throughout the house. Ugh. Looking back, it was horrible. (Living with those colors for a year is probably why I paint every wall a neutral color to this day.) I had my dining room. I had my house. I had my BMW, and I had my own money. As I saw it, I was ahead of the game. My friends in college were going to wait years before they had a house or a high-paying job. Of course, I was slowly realizing that they were going to catch up and maybe even pass me and have really nice houses and jobs with futures. Like every nineteen-year-old, I was starting to face the stark reality of my future.

I enrolled at Hillsborough Community College. I was someone who had breezed through honors classes in high school and I considered myself a bit overqualified for the basic English class that was required. However, I loved the professor. She reminded me of my Gram. She was in her seventies, tall, with short white hair and the posture of a ballet dancer. She had a PhD and was supersmart and pulled together. I was fascinated by this woman. But I was absolutely blown away when my first piece of homework—a simple one-paragraph assignment—came back trashed with red marks.

I remember going to my professor in disbelief and her telling me, "It needs to be better." I was perplexed; I still have a report I wrote in third grade about John Quincy Adams on which my teacher wrote: "Better than most college students'." I'm sure she was just instilling confidence in a child, but teachers take note: That comment made me feel smart, and I still own it! Here I was, a college student, basically being told my essay was as good as something the average third grader would write. Then and there, I realized there's always room for improvement—*always*. I worked hard in that class. I was bound and determined to win her praise. She saw my attitude change and pulled me in for a conference. She asked what my goals were; I said I wanted to find success. I told her I worked at Hooters and went to school part-time because I wanted to make money. She said, "I think you need to work on how you define success and realize that you're not going to get what you want until you hang up those orange shorts." I thought, Oh, ouch. Then, You know what? She's right.

It struck me like a lightning bolt. I didn't have a long-term plan. Her comment stayed with me as I turned a critical eye on my current situation. There was a small group of waitresses at Hooters that the rest of us called "lifers." They were in their late thirties or early forties and had already done a stint at the restaurant when they were my age. Most had gotten married (some to customers) and then after a divorce or a few children, they were back at Hooters because they didn't have a plan B and had never finished school or acquired other job skills. It was sobering to think I was headed down the same path.

Around that time, things with Steve finally came to a head. He sat me down one night for "the talk." It was obvious to both of us that all the work I was doing was a way for me to not be at home or in the relationship. Steve was ready to settle down, get married, and all the rest. I was just realizing that I had a lot to do before I ever "settled down." *If* I ever settled down. I had discovered that I could go it alone. And that was the death of our relationship, right there. I knew what was coming when we sat across from each other in the dining room. But I don't think he did.

"We can't go on like this."

I nodded. "I know."

"We have to make some changes."

I kept nodding. "I know."

"You have to make a decision. You're either in or out."

"You're right." And then I stopped nodding. "So this is what we should do. I'm going to keep the house. You can move out as soon as you find a place and . . ."

Judging from the shocked look on his face, Steve had thought the conversation would go in a different direction. I've always been one of those people who just rips the Band-Aid off. When I make a hard decision, I don't look back. I'm a firm believer that there's no use in second-guessing yourself.

Steve moved out three weeks later, but not before we had a blowout about who would get our brand-new futon. The fight was about much more than the futon, of course, but as I've learned since, arguments are rarely only about the matter at hand. My dad drafted a contract for the house and the futon and I bought Steve out. The house was now mine alone. I was carrying a mortgage by myself. I hadn't really created a formal budget, but it quickly became apparent—between a hefty car payment, living costs, and a mortgage—that I either needed more income or I had to rent out rooms. I'm all about the work, so my ears perked up when one of my Hooters regulars, a sales guy named Jack, gave me some free advice.

"You need to get into outside sales," he told me.

That's what Steve had always done, so I knew the risks.

I shook my head. "I can't do all commission."

He looked at me like I was crazy. "You do commission here every day. You sell a million wings and you get a piece of that. Call it tips; call it commissions. It's the same thing."

It made sense when he put it like that. The next day, I corralled one of my friends at Hooters, a waitress named Kristina. I knew she had been selling cell phones in her free time, and I knew cell phones were high-ticket items that everyone wanted. Kristina said, "Oh sure, it's easy. They sell themselves."

That was pretty much all I needed to hear. I went down and talked to the manager of the company she worked for and convinced him that I could move cell phones (even if I didn't happen to own one yet!). I sold me. He hired me on the spot. That's how I gave up my day shift at Hooters, said good-bye to working grueling doubles, and started filling my days with cold calls convincing people to ride the early wave of the wireless revolution and part with fifteen hundred dollars for a Motorola StarTAC.

I learned that no matter what the situation, you dress the part and get to work. Even though I could work at home, I knew that with this being straight outside sales with no leads, if I didn't take myself seriously, no one would take me seriously. So rather

than make pitches on my own cell phone from the beach, I put on a suit and started visiting businesses. I loved having the freedom of making my own hours, and very soon the commission checks started coming in.

A girlfriend from Hooters moved in because I needed help paying the mortgage. For the first couple of weeks, it was fun having her there. We talked a lot, dreamed aloud, watched movies, and ate bad food. Having a roommate was okay. That is, until I realized I was the only one buying the food. I was also the only one washing dishes, vacuuming, and scrubbing the toilet. And when the rent came due after the very first month, along with the utilities and the cable bill, suddenly the fun stopped and the excuses started. It amazed me that while I was working around the clock juggling cell phones, Hooters wings, and a toilet brush, she was the one who was hard to track down, especially when the bills were due. It took me a while to real-ize that when people owe you money, they will do everything in their power to make *you* out to be the bad guy. I'd like to say I learned that lesson right there, but no, as my Gramps says, you don't let people's ignorance change who you are. Once a giver, always a giver.

So I was about to turn twenty, I was struggling with a hefty mortgage and bills, and I was beat. Cold-calling for commissions can take the wind out of anyone's sails. I couldn't see a light at the end of the tunnel with one community college class at a time either. I began to feel like I was spinning my wheels.

The hardest part was the dawning realization that I was using temporary solutions for long-term challenges. I wanted success and to be self-sufficient. But I wanted it now. So instead of thinking long term—go get a college degree, start my own business, be smart about it—I did everything short term. I worked my butt off at three jobs I didn't particularly like to buy a house for way more than it was worth instead of saving for what I really wanted. Even at twenty I could figure out that if I had done things the right way, by twenty-five I'd have been able to buy the house I really wanted.

That's not the thinking you want to be doing just when you're headed home for a visit. It was my grandparents' fiftieth wedding anniversary and my parents were seeing me at my weakest. There was nothing about my life that made sense to them. They had never been thrilled about me working at Hooters. Even though I had the new prospects of the cell-phone job, they hoped that all my high-school honor roll achievements would lead to a college degree. It's fair to say I was a little vulnerable the day after the party, when I said to them, "I'm thinking of coming home."

Trust, I pulled my words back five seconds later, but my mom heard what she wanted to, and the wheels were in motion. I saw the wisdom in it. I thought, You know what? If I'm so smart, getting a college degree won't slow me down, and it just might help. I flew back to Tampa feeling a little lighter.

But I wasn't ready to sell the house just yet. It was an investment, and it was still important to me that I owned a house. I could always come back. Plus, from time to time, I would trot out the note with the schedule of payments. On the payoff date, I would be twenty-eight years old. The way I saw it, at twenty-eight I would have fifty-eight thousand dollars in the bank! I wasn't about to let that go.

Coincidentally, a friend needed a new place to live. So to kill two birds with one stone, I told him I was moving back to Michigan, and that he could rent my place. This time, though, I bought a standard-form lease and had him read and sign it. That led to my first experience having to evict a tenant. Just like you should never do business with friends or family, you should never rent to them either.

A month later, my mom showed up with my brother and a U-Haul. It was time to go. We packed up my things and I took one last look at the house, with the flowers still in bloom along the front walk and the clean windows sparkling in the sun. Then I crammed myself into the truck's front seat between my mom and my brother and we started the long drive back to Lake Orion. It was another sunny Tampa morning, but I felt a little dark. I tried to focus on what would come next, but the trip made me feel a bit like the wayward daughter slinking home. Halfway to Michigan, I was begging my mom to let me unhitch my car and drive home by myself. She wasn't having it. I think she figured I might try a break for the coast.

I had a lot to think about on that long drive. But only over time would I understand the lessons the house on West Pearl Avenue taught me.

The wrong house can be worse than no house at all. Just like the right job is the one you decide you'll take, instead of letting circumstances or other people's expectations choose for you. You really have to think long term, in life as well as with houses. I had bought a house someone had flipped, and I'd gotten stung for it.

Now no matter how quickly I plan on turning a house, I always ask myself a question: If you couldn't sell it, would you live in it? If you can see yourself living in a house for the foreseeable future—having a good life there and making pleasant memories—chances are other people will, too. Houses flipped only for profit are rarely about quality, and that's what I want in my life and my work: quality. That's why that house was so wrong. It just wasn't quality.

So, no, the Tampa house was never a good long-term solution, but it was a place to make some cheap mistakes and learn valuable lessons. It's where I discovered that it's wise to know what you're doing before you launch into a project. Understand value in everything you do. I also learned what I don't want in life: throwaway things. Cars that don't matter. Relationships that don't matter. And houses that have no value. I learned that I had to plan a little more, both in life and in renovating houses.

Within a couple of years, the house would be gone, the BMW would be gone, and most of my Hooters money would be gone. But the lessons that house in Tampa taught me would remain. That house may have been a mistake, but it was anything but a failure. It didn't make me money, but it gave me knowledge that I would use as a mother, a businesswoman, a friend, and a person. This is what I tell people when they beat themselves up about taking a chance that didn't work out. You got a gift. Failure teaches so much more than success. Don't avoid your failures; turn them into assets by taking away essential life lessons. You'll be happier if you look at things that way. I don't worry about the Tampa house, and I've long forgotten the mistakes of that time. But all those valuable lessons? Thank goodness, they're with me still.

# Chapter 2

# YOU CAN'T ALWAYS CHOOSE WHAT YOU KEEP, BUT YOU CAN CHOOSE WHAT YOU LET GO

## MINNEHAHA HOUSE

Coming back to Michigan from Tampa was a journey into both the past and the future. I'd be lying if I said it didn't feel a little defeating to move back into my parents' tri-level, open-floor-plan home (with no place to hide except in my bedroom). It was tough for everyone. I had lived on my own and I was a landlord with my own little ranch in Tampa. But my parents still thought of me as the high school teenager I had been when I left, right down to the eleven o'clock curfew and the list of chores. I stayed focused on the future. For me, that was all about regrouping, getting myself through college, and starting my career.

Bartending at the Fox and Hounds.

All that—and getting my own place—was going to take money. Within a couple of weeks of coming back from Tampa, I had applied at the Fox and Hounds, an upscale restaurant outside of Detroit. When I left Hooters I was working as a bartender, but at the time, Hooters served only beer and wine. The manager who hired me in Detroit didn't realize this, and knowing I would make more money as a bartender than as a server, I didn't correct him. On my first day, I was thrown right into the fire bartending a wedding. People were asking me to make Greyhounds, Rusty Nails, and Old-Fashioneds. The good thing is that when alcohol is free, people are very forgiving. More than once, I would ask, "Tell me how you like yours made." Those wedding guests gave me a quick education. And I decided to find a shoulder to cry on about my lost independence in Steve, who had moved back to Michigan as well, and as a former bartender, he helped me get up to speed. It was important to me that I master this job, as insignificant as bartending may seem to some (mostly to those who have never done it). I like to be perfect at every job I try. I was serving the who's who of Michigan, and I definitely wanted to make a good impression; breaking off a cork in a two-hundred-dollar bottle of wine or ruining a hundred-dollar pour of Louis XIII cognac was not the way to do it. I saw the opportunity in having close contact with Detroit's elite. Most people have to compete for an intern position with such high-powered CEOs; I just had to learn the ins and outs of cigars and how to pour a proper drink. And no one loves to tell you what you need to do to succeed like ego-driven CEOs. I soaked up every last detail, and came to the conclusion that even though I wanted to go my own direction, I would still benefit from having a college degree.

I was done with plugging away at college one class at a time. I was miserable living at my parents' house and thought if I was going to put myself through this, I might as well put my nose to the grindstone. I took a full class load and then some at the community college. I worked around the clock and kept reminding myself that in the end, it would all be worth it. It's the same mentality I use when I'm running to get from mile one all the way to the end. If you are going to do it, just get it done. The best way to get through hell is to keep on moving. And sometimes that means literally moving— I moved back in with Steve.

My newfound plan was proceeding nicely. But as you've probably heard before, one way to make God laugh is to make a plan. Just into the spring, Steve and I found out that I was pregnant. I was twenty, which seems so young to me now, but my mom had me when she was seventeen. I would be twenty-one by the time the baby was born, so it seemed right on time. I was feeling excited and scared, and most of all blessed. I grew up in an extended family with a lot of children; I loved kids, and Steve was excited too. He and I might have faltered before, but I felt that we had found our way and we truly loved each other.

But now my plan needed some adjusting. Bartending and going to school full-time was no longer viable. Something had to give. The other challenge was that Steve had to fulfill a contract out of town beginning when I was just three months into my pregnancy. I put on a brave face. I pulled together an impressive résumé and interviewed for a job as a key accounts representative at a cell phone company. What was that? I had no idea, but I figured I had mastered cell phone sales before, so there was only one thing that was going to happen: I had to get that job. After the owners hired me—offering an impressive salary of thirty thousand dollars a year plus commissions—they looked at me and asked, "How old are you?" I told them I was twenty, and I could see from the look on their faces that they were thinking, What have we done? There's something that happens when you come across obstacles: You either learn to jump through the hoops or you stumble and land on your face. I assured them that they could hire someone older with more experience, but not someone with more drive. I gave my notice at the Fox and Hounds and threw myself into school and my new job.

It was a difficult time and I missed Steve like crazy, but every day that beautiful baby moved inside me, I knew I was taking on the role I felt destined for: Mom.

I remember celebrating my twenty-first birthday and my Gram hugging me and saying everything was going to be okay. It was just a few months before Ethan would be born, and my wonderful Gram sensed my worry. I leaned into that hug and cried my eyes out. I just needed reassurance, and I always found it in her arms.

The next few months flew by, and before I knew it, I was walking out of the hospital with Ethan in my arms. Oh, how I had never known such love. I was so happy with that little baby in my life. Tired. Exhausted. But filled with joy. However, the one thing I lacked at twenty-one was faith in my parental instincts—I was leery of trusting my gut. Everyone had an opinion about what I was supposed to do, and how I was supposed to raise Ethan. All that unasked-for advice can prey on you, and it sapped my energy.

If only I could go back and talk to young Nicole, I'd tell her, "Take a deep breath and relax."

Soon I was back at work. I would've loved to stay home and be with Ethan all day, but Steve was still gone and we needed my income. It killed me to drop him off at day care early in the morning and not see him again until early evening. Even worse, my idealistic vision of balancing work, baby, breast-feeding, and home life all quickly vanished. There is nothing more heartbreaking than having a breast pump connected to you in a

dirty bathroom stall rather than having your darling infant at your breast. All of this led to more than just a mere resentment of Steve's absence. When Steve returned to Michigan, I was able to quit my job, yet we struggled to adjust. I wasn't used to having a party of three, and quite honestly, he wasn't used to living a life where family took priority. He had been living like a bachelor and I had been living like a single mom those first few months after Ethan's birth. Even though we were moments away from moving into our new house on a lake—which, to my surprise, I had been able to finance on

Ethan's first Easter.

my own—and seemed to have everything going for us on the outside, on the inside it was daily arguing and conflict. I was all of twenty-one years old, but I knew I just wanted a healthy home environment in which to raise this child and I couldn't quiet the nagging feeling that maybe the best way to provide it was to be on my own.

When Steve left for a work trip, I packed what I could into a few suitcases and left. I took refuge in an empty apartment on my grandparents' property. It was far from glamorous, and it was most humbling to give up a beautiful home on a lake and everything that life was supposed to entail, but the truth was, I was broke. The apartment had been occupied by any number of my family members at one time or another when life smacked them upside the head, and now it was my turn. I took some time to figure out how to get back on track. I couldn't return to a nine-to-five job and go to school at the same time. It just wouldn't work. So I put my ego aside and went back to bartending. I felt like I was back at square one. It wasn't easy and I ate more twenty-five-cent potpies than I care to admit, all while Steve was living in our lake house, driving a Mercedes, and making more money than we had ever imagined. I was living in seven hundred square feet of space. I painted the place and did the best I could with nothing but scraps of this and that, but to add insult to injury, my new living room had to house that damn futon from West Pearl Avenue. Looking back, I have no idea where my courage to leave came from, but it doesn't matter. When my days are difficult now, I think back to those moments in the small apartment. It was there—out of pure desperation—that I knew I had to end that relationship in order to find a path forward. Having nothing and being at your lowest point tends to make you creative.

I transferred to a four-year college to get my teaching degree and was taking a full class load. But when I was unable to get a sitter on New Year's Eve, I was fired from my bartending job. I was devastated; I had just started

Our time in the Indian Lake Road back apartment.

A proud moment: my baby and my first (and only) business vehicle.

to get back on my feet. A friend who pulled no punches said, "It's the best thing that has ever happened to you; you are never going to focus on getting what you want when you're secure in what you have." In other words, the bartending was paying the bills and I was getting comfortable with it and losing sight of my goal to work for myself. That week, I did what I do best: I created a new avenue. I sat down and made up cleaning flyers. I had to find work, and it had to be more flexible than just some nine-to-five job or another bartending gig.

The next day, I popped Ethan into a baby carrier, hoisted it onto my back, and started pounding the pavement. I went to every nearby apartment complex and rubber banded the flyers to doorknobs. Within two weeks, I had enough jobs to fill my calendar.

I saw cleaning houses as my gold mine. My mind is like a spreadsheet at all times. I got it down to a science. I knew how many pieces of paper towel it took for each house, how many ounces of Windex. I knew to the penny what my overhead was and I soon realized that by hiring someone to work with me, I could double my client list. All the while, those college credits were adding up, and I was finally able to take my teaching certification exam.

I passed. And while that should have been my moment of feeling accomplished, I was faced with the reality that if I went on to finish my teaching degree and do the required student teaching (with six months of no pay), I would ultimately come out making a third of what I was making cleaning houses. Looking back, I realize I was a bit short-sighted. But at that moment, I had a little boy who I wanted to make sure had everything his heart desired, and that meant a house, a backyard, and Disney vacations. I made the decision to put off school right then and there. With school off my calendar, I doubled my business.

In no time at all—well, fifteen months in that back apartment—with money I had saved up and the proceeds of the sale of the Tampa house, I bought a fabulous 1928 bungalow in Ferndale, an up-and-coming suburb of Detroit. The house needed work, but I didn't care. I ripped into it with a newfound passion, uncovering all the beautiful features of an old house. I tore out the outdated carpeting and walked on the original oak floors; I peeled back the vinyl wallpaper and applied fresh paint on plaster.

Our first Christmas photo in front of the Ferndale house (top). Ethan playing dress-up in our new home (bottom).

Ethan was always by my side working with his smock on.

Ethan was so excited working alongside me. We didn't have much, but I was so proud to finally own a home again. I remember one time saying to Steve how tired I was from working on the house, and that it must be nice being able to pay someone to do everything. (He had moved nearby, and had the money to hire someone to work on his house.) He replied, "You wouldn't have it any other way." He was right. Those days are so vivid in my mind.

The redesign of the Ferndale house along with years of knowing hundreds of different homes intimately through cleaning them led me to offer unsolicited design ideas to my clients. I would see the money they were paying designers for designs that just weren't feasible or sustainable. So with many houses, I would leave sketches along with an appointment card only to see on my next visit that they had been tossed in the garbage. After all, I was just the housecleaner. Still, I was finding that my hunger for design

The simple life: renovating and having fun with Ethan.

Ethan during our Ferndale years.

was growing each day. I placed an ad on Craigslist offering design services for free if I could photograph the work and add it to my portfolio. And this is why I laugh now when people ask me how they can do what I do designing homes. I always say, "Work for free." I've never been formally trained in interior design. Some in the field will say that it shows, and that's okay. I actually like not going by anything other than my gut instinct. When you don't have an example of what to do, everything you do is original. I laugh now looking back—in six years at my Ferndale house, I accomplished what I can now do in three weeks. We made so many memories in that little home. While I was obsessing over the historical renovation, I was also adding my own design. I took three months painting a Spider-Man mural for Ethan in his room, only to have the little guy look up at me and say, "I don't think

I like Spider-Man anymore, Mommy," after I finished. Of all my houses, I still know every square inch of that one, and I can't help but recall all the hours spent working on it and the little moments when Ethan thought I needed a pick-me-up and would appear out of nowhere in his kangaroo suit just to make me laugh.

Ethan went from being a stumbling toddler to starting kindergarten. Time was flying by. I can't express how grateful I am to have recognized early on that this was the best time of my life. I wouldn't start my workday until after dropping off E at school, and I would finish by the time he was done. I didn't care if I was scrubbing someone else's toilets, it was giving me the freedom I wanted as a mom and financial stability.

Steve and me taking Ethan on a family vacation (left).
Ethan and me in California visiting Steve (right).

Party of three: Polly, Ethan, and me.

There was also a lot of growing up and change going on outside of that home. Steve and I struggled for many years to find our way when it came to shared parenting. Even though I was convinced that my being on my own would bring us peace, the relationship went from bad to worse. I hadn't planned on a custody battle that involved lawyers, court dates, and strangers having an opinion about our parenting. Luckily, we came to our senses and realized that this fight wasn't about a meaningless futon—it was about our baby. We went from being the couple who exchanged the baby at the police station to the family at Disney World together. It wasn't perfect, but we had a good run for a long time. And there was no "his time" or "my time," just Ethan's time.

As Ethan was entering second grade, Steve made the difficult decision to accept a job in California. Before moving, he took Ethan away for a long weekend and I found myself home alone with the two dogs, Polly and Max. (A lesson to all parents: If you take your cute little boy to "look" at dogs, you will come home with a dog, or maybe even two.) I'm not someone who normally needs a night out. But my friend Rick, knowing that Ethan was away with his dad, called and said he and some friends were going to a club called Temple. I told him I might swing by. I was worn out from a hectic week and missing Ethan. I really just wanted to distract myself by cleaning my house and maybe reorganizing my already organized closet. However, at 9 P.M., I got my second wind. I decided, What the heck? I'll go out for a bit.

Temple was an upscale restaurant that switched over into a trendy dance club at night. The place was hopping when I walked through the door. Rick was nowhere to be found, and my anxiety set in. I found myself standing at the bar wishing I were back at home. The DJ was spinning, and I was right next to the dance floor, which was dotted with large, lighted Plexiglas cubes that anyone could get up on and dance. Standing on one put you front and center; if you were dancing on one of them, you were either the most secure person in the world or just really drunk.

I watched as a boyishly handsome guy walked by. He was dressed well, with the clean-cut good looks of a frat boy. Suddenly, a girl jumped down from one of the cubes and collided with him. The guy went flying, ending up sprawled on his butt right in front of me. He let out a shout of surprise and looked up at me.

"I saw the whole thing. A clear case of assault. I'll testify," I offered. He laughed as I helped him up.

That's how I met Christopher; I didn't know it then, but that night out would lead to *Rehab Addict*. After he dusted himself off, he offered to buy me a drink. I said no thanks, that I was actually getting ready to leave as soon as I could find my friends. So he ordered a beer and we started talking. He was funny, and to be honest, I was quite proud of myself for being out and not at home curled up with Max and Polly. His friends joined us. I hung out with them until about one in the morning. As everyone was getting ready to go, Christopher and I were waiting for the valet and he still hadn't asked for my number. So I took the initiative and said, "Are you going to ask me for my number or what?" Even as in my head I heard my Gramps saying, "Never chase the man." Christopher looked shocked and said, "I didn't think you were interested in me. Of course I want your number."

Christopher and I shared ambition and an abundance of energy. It was clear from the start that we were both risk takers. While I was starting my businesses and being a mom, he was out traveling the world. He had been valedictorian of his high school class and had earned an MBA after graduating from an Ivy League college, which made him believe he was guaranteed success. The most successful people I knew did not have an MBA—they had street smarts. But I was still intrigued by his drive.

Ironically, just as Christopher and I started hitting our groove, he was offered a really great position with a company in Minneapolis. He asked me if I wanted to move with him. We had had a great first six months. Ethan got along well with Christopher. The dogs liked him, and I felt like we had the same goal of eventually working for ourselves. Looking back, we were both a bit naive. Had we left it there, gone our separate ways, I think we would have remained good friends. But I've always been a romantic, and you read enough stories about people who meet, fall in love, and are married happily

We moved in October; Ethan and Polly had fun in the leaves in our
Southwest Minneapolis home.

ever after that you start to think: Why am I fighting this? By then, Steve was living in California, and with everything going on with Detroit, I thought this was something I should just go with. Plus, Christopher made me laugh. So off we went. The plan was to spend eighteen months in Minneapolis, save money, and then head to California.

Our first Halloween in Minneapolis.

We rented a house in Southwest Minneapolis, and I was pretty confident that I would be able to find a "career" quickly, with all the companies headquartered in the city. I loved being a team, dropping E off at his new school, volunteering, cooking dinner, and just relaxing for a moment. The job leads led to dead ends. But I was happy to just be able to focus on being a mom, planning parties, attending field trips, and doing my best to make sure that E was happy and making friends. As the mother of an only child, you constantly feel that your child is missing out. Ethan didn't have a sibling to play with, so I looked for opportunities for him to meet other kids. Being a baseball fan, I had always helped with his Little League teams in Michigan. So in Minneapolis I joined forces with some great people to coach baseball. But while I was quite content being a stay-at-home mom, Christopher was all about dual incomes. I found a random job as an international relocation assistant. I was in charge of helping foreign executives adapt to living in Minnesota, which gave us a good laugh because I was new to Minneapolis myself and I was being paid to teach people about the city. My clients were from all over the world, and E was as fascinated with their stories as I was. The idea that they had thrown caution to the wind and gone to a foreign country made me a little more accepting of my failures in securing what I thought of as real work. I had my fill of cleaning houses after a decade and decided to focus on design in Minneapolis. I was still trying my hardest to attract new design clients—anything to avoid a "real" job that would require me to be somewhere from nine to five. But I quickly found that "Minnesota nice" meant someone would say, "I'd love to work with you; let me get your number," and then never call. I was getting my first taste of passive-aggressive behavior, and it was rough.

At one point, convinced I would be hired for a commercial design position, I was shocked to hear the young human resources recruiter tell me, "You're just not a good fit for us." I called Christopher crying, and he said, "Maybe you aren't." I was pissed. That day he did something that would change the course of my life—he made a call to a real estate broker we had been working with to find a house. He told me that night, "I signed you up to get your real estate license." Knowing Christopher, it was certainly more financially driven than supportive. But it made me ask, Why didn't I do this sooner? Being a real estate agent was a natural next step. I knew the ins and outs from my own property investments, and I knew renovation and design, so I could offer that insight. Most of all, my part-time gig as a relocation assistant proved more than anything that I had the skills to help people find a home. But I hadn't really thought of it as a lucrative career. The few times I had worked with real estate agents, I had been frustrated because they did little more than let me into a house so that I could look around. I had done sales all my life. I knew I could move houses and do a whole lot more than turn a key. But more important, Christopher pointed out, "Nic, one house nets you 2.7 percent of the sales price. Do the math! It takes you two or three clients to make that now."

It all made sense. The next week, I dropped E off at school and went to get my real estate license. Sitting in classes for three weeks, I wanted to kick myself for not having done it years earlier and for all the money I had missed out on.

The Minneapolis real estate market was on fire. We were bursting at the seams in our rental, and it was driving me nuts that I couldn't even paint a wall. For six months, we got outbid on houses. We were used to "Detroit prices," as one person put it after Christopher and I complained about getting outbid on yet another house. A house would go on the market and by noon, there would be multiple offers. The stress of all that and the arguments over money were too much. I had always been independent, but at the same time, I always did and still do think of the man as the provider. Christopher didn't see it that way. Just as all hell was about to break loose, we had the winning offer on our Yellow house and our energy and our relationship were renewed. The day we won the bid, we were offered twenty thousand dollars to walk away. I was shocked and saddened when we couldn't find another house to buy. Can you imagine making twenty thousand dollars in one day? I was intrigued. If the market was this crazy, Christopher and I knew we had to get going. The house was a foreclosure and a mess.

I was working full-time in real estate and renovating our house at the same time.

Ethan Rollerblading in the new house.

It wasn't pretty, but I spent a week cleaning and painting getting ready for us to move in. Ethan was excited about the new place and took much joy in being able to Rollerblade through the empty house.

We moved on Easter weekend of 2008. Easter is a spring holiday, but what we soon learned about Minneapolis is that it has two seasons: summer and winter. We ended up moving in a foot of snow.

From March 2008 to June 2009, I was hustling real estate and renovating the Yellow house. Christopher was devoting more and more hours to work; every day he'd come home and I'd have one project completed and another new idea in the works. Ethan loved being in the city—we were within walking distance of the lakes, and he had many new friends in the neighborhood.

Our house was in a section of the city called Uptown, and everything else—Ethan's school and my office—was in our old neighborhood. Every day, I drove by a 1916 Arts and Crafts mansion on Minnehaha Parkway. The house had seen better days, but I knew that it could be stunning. The architectural style was more Santa Monica than Minneapolis. It had a Spanish clay tile roof, tons of large windows, and a stacked stone foundation and entryway surround. It had

Ethan steering our canoe through Lake Calhoun.

such potential. The problem was, it wasn't for sale. Even if it had been, I didn't think we could have afforded it. As the months clicked by, we finished the Yellow house, adding a master suite and restoring every inch of it. Once we finished, I was eager to invest in another house. I found the perfect candidate: a fixer-upper on Grand Avenue. I called it the 20K house because that's what it cost. I made the owners an offer on the low end of reasonable, which was what we could afford. The offer was refused. It was summer vacation, so I scooped up Ethan and my dogs, Max and Polly, and drove to Michigan in our old Ranger pickup truck. These days you won't catch me on a road trip, but back then it cost a thousand dollars to fly and a couple hundred bucks and two days to drive. I had more time than money, so road trip it was.

To be honest, as much as I was rocking out in Minneapolis, I was starting to think it was time to reconsider Detroit. I knew I could sell our Yellow house fast, and I was pretty sure Christopher would be just fine being a bachelor again. Once I was back in Michigan, I could see that there was actually a lot of opportunity for me to jump into real estate in Detroit. Ethan stayed on a little longer in Michigan. I was back in Minneapolis and had pretty

The Minnehaha house exterior, before (top) and after (bottom) renovations.

Many years of Christmas photos taken at our Yellow house.

much decided to bail. I was headed down Lyndale Avenue to check in at my office when God intervened.

I noticed a bright red-and-white For Sale sign on Minnehaha's front lawn. I pulled over and called Christopher. He didn't answer. I'm known for long-winded voice mails (even though the voice mail on my own phone was always exclusively for my grandparents; everyone else knows I won't listen to their messages, and my voice mail doesn't even have a greeting).

My voice mails are most of the time not even intelligible. When I get excited about something, like my dream home hitting the market, it's a mixture of screams, probably a "holy shit," and more screams. So I said, "This is so awesome. Okay, okay, call me back!"

The house was wide open and people were walking in and out. A property in that neighborhood on the market in foreclosure was rare, so people were drawn to it like a moth to a flame—it was going to be hot.

As soon as I got inside the house, I fell even more in love. Everywhere you looked, there was stunning original woodwork and space galore. The house had windows upon windows that brought in tons of light and air. But even for me, the amount of work Minnehaha would require was staggering. The last owner, before it had been foreclosed on, had lived in the house for a year without water or heat. Therefore, almost every wall was severely cracked. Everything in the house was shot. The basement was the worst part. It was flooded and had been for a long time. It was so murky down there that it was actually scary. I didn't care. I knew it was just a matter of a lot of hard work to turn the house into a unique treasure, a standout in the Minneapolis landscape. Plus, all the damage inside was scaring off other potential buyers. I heard people saying, "Well, we'd just need to tear it down and build something new on the lot." Horrified at that thought, I called Christopher and left another message, saying, "This is it!" As much as we had our differences, Christopher knew that if I said "This is it!" I was usually right.

Apparently, every other savvy investor thought Minnehaha was a hot mess and no one put in an offer. I told Christopher, "I'm either a genius or an idiot." There are only a few people who see the advantage of risk, and I'm one of them. Christopher and I put in an offer, and the bank actually came back with a lower number. I still don't understand why, but I've never been one to look a gift horse in the mouth. We just moved ahead.

The Minnehaha kitchen, before (top); Ethan checking out the progress (bottom, left);
and the same kitchen, after (bottom, right).

A few days later, the agent for the Grand Avenue house called. The buyer who had outbid me had lost his financing. That house was mine, too, if I could still swing it. I thought, This is it. Sink or swim, Nic. I can't swim, but I think as long as you manage to keep your head above water, that's good enough. So I told Christopher, "Let's do both."

It was not going to be easy. Between the two properties, we would need about one hundred thousand dollars in cash: twenty thousand to buy the Grand Avenue house, and eighty thousand for the down payment on Minnehaha. We created a spreadsheet of everyone we knew who might loan us money. We decided to refinance my Ferndale house to get the twenty thousand dollars for the Grand Avenue house (aka the 20K house). Then we called everyone we could and put together the down payment for Minnehaha bit by bit. It still wasn't a done deal, but I said, "If it works, I stay. If it doesn't, I'm going back to Detroit."

I headed to my office to send over the offers on both houses. The receptionist casually said, "Nicole, you know your office voice mail is full?" I didn't even know I had office voice mail; I always gave out my cell number. One message in particular caught my attention. It was from a production assistant for Magnetic Productions. He said he wanted to line up real estate experts who could go on camera for segments on a TV show.

The message was two weeks old. I sat there shaking my head. Leave it to me not to check my messages. I called the guy back and, to my surprise, he told me to come in the next day.

The next morning, I pitched a couple of ideas aloud, using my dogs, Max and Polly, as my audience. A very successful friend of mine from years back always told me to practice aloud before speaking to others so that it wouldn't be startling for me to hear my own voice (and if you lose your audience, to smile and say "God bless America"—you always end with cheers). So there I was with Max and Polly. Remember, I was the little bookworm girl whom no one expected a peep out of, and then . . . I got my voice. Psyching myself up was nothing new. For years, I played the flute in school, and every week someone could challenge me for my seat. I wanted to be first chair, which was the "best" player. I traded the chair with another girl from week to week. I would come in with my band book covered in stickies with acronyms: YCDI ("You can do it."). When the time came to perform for the chair, I'd look down at those notes and think, Hell yeah, I got this. I'm pretty sure my parents let me know that in twenty years no one would remember if I was first chair or last, but—aha!—I remember, and for the most part, I was first chair.

As I was leaving the house, I thought, if I'm going in to talk to somebody about a TV show, I'm going to walk out of there with my own TV show. I should note that I'd had a Coke for breakfast. This thought wasn't so much overconfidence as it was something I call "caffeine courage." I'm already a high-energy person, and the caffeine took it to another level. By the time I arrived at Magnetic Productions in the cool, historic North Loop downtown, I was on fire. I wasn't a huge TV person. In fact, I'm that parent who believes "screen time" is bad. We didn't have a TV in the house until Ethan was five, but I knew enough to know that no one on TV was celebrating the kind of home improvement I did.

I was met at the door by the production assistant, and he started sizing up my qualifications right away.

"Tell me about your experiences as a realtor."

"You know, I'm not just a realtor. I'm also an investor and I renovate homes," I told him, and launched into my spiel: I save old houses. I do a lot of the work myself. I do this and I do that.

"No way."

"Yep."

He looked at me for a second, like he was deciding something. Then he left the room and came back with John Kitchener, the owner of the company. John is a tall, slim man—Steve Jobs without the glasses. I would later find out that he was a cancer survivor, and I think that contributed to his no-nonsense, straight-shooting demeanor. He came in, introduced himself, and gave me a puzzled look. "Wait a minute, now, tell me what you do?"

I told him that my goal was to invest in the houses that no one else wanted, renovate them in a historic manner, and put them back on the market. I told him about my Ferndale house and my Yellow house.

John said, "What do you mean—you're flipping?"

"Well, technically, yes. But flipping isn't really what I do. I bring the houses back to life, leaving their integrity intact."

He said, "No one is flipping; it's dead. All those shows have been canceled." (John was correct. This was 2009, and the housing market was in terrible shape. All the HGTV shows were about design, not real estate ventures.)

This business card photo led to my days (years) on *Rehab Addict*.

The painted archway in the basement, before (left), and the finished basement, after (right).

I said to him, "Not in Minneapolis; this market is hot."

"So you do the work." He rubbed his forehead. To be fair, I didn't look like someone who would ever think of breaking a nail, let alone getting dirty. I was wearing high heels and my favorite black suit with a vest instead of a jacket, and my hair was down. "You do drywall, you do plumbing, like all of that?"

"Yeah, I've learned to do it all."

"All right, so if we showed up with a camera tomorrow, you'd be working on a house?"

"Yeah, of course."

"You know what? You need your own show."

"Yeah, I probably do," I said with a smirk.

The assistant, still standing there looking for a consultant for his project, which I found out was *Sweat Equity*, wasn't quite sure what had just happened. "Should I book her for *Sweat Equity*?"

According to Ethan, there's no resemblance at all. Hmmm.

John said, "No, she's not doing *Sweat Equity*. We're going to do a show about her." I actually ended up doing a cameo on *Sweat Equity* when they were in a pinch for a guest realtor later on after I had my show. I never saw it—my friends told me, "Don't watch it; you were horrible in realtor mode."

When people ask how I got my show, I tell them about everything that led me to it: the house going up for sale, and the random production assistant scanning the Internet for a TV-ready realtor for a cameo finding my absolutely terrible website photo. But most of all, I talk about being in the right place at the right time. John had just started the company. Production companies make their money by producing shows and selling them to networks. He had run Edelman Productions for years, but the company had just closed its office in Minneapolis to focus on the West Coast. John took over the contract for *Sweat Equity* and started out on his own. But that's all he had—a few episodes of one show that might not get renewed, which is not exactly enough to keep an entire company afloat.

John needed new shows to sell, and he was hungry. That's where luck came in. Companies like his succeed only by throwing ideas at the network and seeing what sticks. I was determined to make the idea of Nicole Curtis, historic home renovator, stick.

I called Christopher and told him to meet me for dinner at my favorite Italian restaurant downtown. While I waited for Christopher, I couldn't contain myself. You have to share good news, but I'm superstitious to a fault. I sent a text to my friend Keith: "I don't want to jinx myself, but I just had an interview with a production company and they want to shoot a show about me." He wrote back, "That's awesome." I replied, "No jinxes. I just needed to tell somebody. We're not going to talk about it. We're never going to bring it up. " And, true to my word, we never did until I had a signed contract.

When Christopher sat down and heard what had happened, he got fired up. He had on his marketing guy hat and was thinking a mile a minute.

"This is fantastic. You can be a brand, like Martha Stewart. We can flip houses and get them press so that we can sell them for top dollar. We can build a business off this. What are we going to do for a house?"

"We can use the Grand Avenue house."

The Grand Avenue house (not to be confused with my future Detroit Grand Boulevard house) hadn't been worked on in maybe sixty years. Anything that had been done was pretty much a combination of duct tape and contact paper. The woman who had lived there since the 1940s had been moved to a nursing home. It was like a time capsule. In fact, Martha, the next-door neighbor, who was in her nineties, had been born right in her house. Two lifers on this street that had seen better days. I was determined to bring back those better days to Grand Avenue. The buyer who had outbid me had plans to tear down this skinny little house. The Grand Avenue house needed *everything* done to it, and it would

Sarah, Keith, and me (left). Me and Keith (right).

be the first house I saved from demolition. While renovating the Yellow house, I had found a carpenter on Craigslist to help me with projects. Slade showed up with a truck full of tools and a zest for old woodwork that matched mine. I called him in on the Grand project, along with a painter I had met. Thinking back to my housecleaning days, I knew I would make more money if I actually hired extra help. We would restore the house inside two months, and have it sold in three.

It seemed like the perfect candidate for a TV show. In TV it's all about the ugly duckling turning into a beautiful swan. And even though I thought it was a beautiful house, it looked like everyone else's worst nightmare. Christopher and I talked all through dinner. By the time we left, we had a whole business model built around the possibility of this show. It was never about people recognizing me; I saw the show as a cash cow, a way to pay for Ethan's college education.

The next day, I got a call from Mary Kay Reistad, a producer at Magnetic. She wanted to make a short video to pitch my show to networks. Mary Kay gave me a brief introduction about how it worked and what I needed to do on camera. The cameraman followed me as I did my first walk-and-talk. I used it as a chance to clearly state my personal mission, which would become the driving vision behind *Rehab Addict*.

"I've always seen the integrity in old homes. I don't want to go in and just slap together a renovation. I don't want to do houses like everyone else does them. I want to celebrate what is unique about any house. My biggest pet peeve is when I look at houses that have been renovated and they all look the same. When people walk into one of my houses, I want them to be like, 'Wow, this is perfect!' I want them to understand what is so special about a historical structure, especially an old house."

I had never filmed anything like it. After a few runs, it felt natural. I just talked to the camera like I would talk to anyone about what I love. If you are truly knowledgeable and passionate about a subject, it comes easy. After they filmed the segment, Mary Kay wanted some action sequences. She asked me if I could do some work on my next house. I took her and the cameraman over to the Grand Avenue house—which we hadn't even started to work on—and did some demolition in the upstairs closet. The shot eventually made it into what became the opening credits for *Rehab Addict*. It's a quick shot, but it goes to show how green I was. I had worn a little red T-shirt and my belly button was exposed—on camera. Lesson learned; enter long black tank tops.

Things moved quickly. We shot the reel, and Mary Kay and her cameraman left. I was on pins and needles.

Summer was over, so I went back to Detroit to get Ethan, feeling much more secure in Minneapolis than I had been at the beginning of the summer and excited about the new possibility of the TV show. Returning home, what did I hear from Mary Kay and John? Nothing . . . just crickets.

Being superstitious, I didn't want to call them and jinx things. I tried my best to just put it to bed and not think about it. I had a lot going on. So I focused on getting Ethan up to speed in school, running around like crazy showing houses, and starting work on the 20K house. After a couple of months, I figured, Okay, having a show wasn't meant to be. I'm not going to stress out about that. But then I got an e-mail from Mary Kay saying, "We're shopping it around and we'll let you know if and when we hear something." Hope has a way of flaring up like a fire you thought had gone out. In spite of myself, I started thinking about the show, and dreaming of everything I could do with it. Still, I heard nothing and just went back to work.

The house was a lot of fun to renovate. When we first arrived, a family of squirrels was living in the ceiling. When we went outside, they would run outside and throw nuts at us. Squirrels are territorial. They didn't care that I held the deed. I was in their space. We discovered a nest of babies that were in danger from the ceiling crashing in. So one day Slade crawled into the attic and caught the squirrels. He said, "Nicole, I have to throw them down to you." I ran upstairs, held out my shirt like a safety net, and safely caught each of the babes. As an animal lover, I would never disturb nature, but had we left them, the squirrels would have died. Slade had made a huge cage for them, and his wife and kids were very excited to have the squirrels at their house for a while before releasing them into the wild. I think of moments like this when people say, "Oh, you flip houses" (as if it's that easy). Ethan came by every day after school, and we set up a cardboard box in the dining room and ate dinner there every night.

Summer soon turned to fall, and the house was done in record time. I took some quick photos and listed the house on Craigslist and MLS at

At the 20K house, Ethan was part of my crew.

the same time. The next morning, as I was driving Ethan to school, I got a call from a buyer who asked me if I could show the house in an hour. He said, "I hope you don't have any offers, because I'm a cash buyer and I'm pretty sure I want it." I thought this was too good to be true. After all, it was a buyer from Craigslist. I dropped Ethan off and drove to the house. The buyer had been in the house for only five minutes when he said, "Would you take five thousand dollars less for a cash deal?" Yeah, yeah I would. Just like that, my twenty-thousand-dollar historical investment house was sold. That little house proved what everyone else didn't believe: There was a market for restored old homes that didn't have open-concept floor plans or granite counters. The neighborhood I loved so much wasn't lost; indeed, it was ready for a comeback.

Right as I sold the house, I got an e-mail from John Kitchener. "We're sorry. We tried. We took it to HGTV, and they don't want it." He sent me a promo of the show the network *had* picked up, *Tough as Nails*. It was disheartening, not only to miss out on the opportunity, but more so because I truly believed there was a need for a show about historic houses. The one they chose was just more of the same— new construction. I accepted that my show wasn't meant to be.

I didn't have a TV show, but I was on top of the world with the sale of the 20K house. I was hungry and I wanted more. While we had been working on that house, we had also closed on Minnehaha. Work there was slow and steady; nothing could be done on the inside until everything structural was done on the outside. We had different subcontractors working on that, and I was focused on selling houses to pay for all the work. I came across a great deal, another foreclosure on Lyndale Avenue. Christopher and I did the numbers and thought, Why not? The profit from a quick redo and sale on that house would help speed up the remodel of Minnehaha. We would have to finance the Lyndale house, and we were in the process of setting that up when another agent in my office asked me to consult with her clients. They were a middle-aged couple who wanted to get into flipping houses. The agent had shown them several houses and nothing had panned out. I met with them, and after a long discussion, they offered to be my investors on Lyndale. Christopher and I discussed it, and we agreed that it was a good way to get moving on the property.

I was so busy at the time—getting the Lyndale deal together, preparing for everything that needed to be done on Minnehaha, and selling houses— that sometimes I wouldn't check my phone until I walked through the door at the end of a long day. One Thursday I got home about seven at night. I walked into my dining room and took off my jacket, dropped my bag on the table, and checked my phone. There was a whole series of missed calls, all from the same number. I recognized it—Magnetic Productions.

I rang John Kitchener and got a warm greeting. "Nicoooollle!"

"Hi, John."

"I sold your show today."

"You what?"

"I sold your show."

"You're kidding me."

"Nope. We need to start filming right away. Are you still working on the Grand Avenue house?"

I told him about the Lyndale house and he said, "That sounds great. Mary Kay will call to set up a shoot schedule." A shoot schedule? We hadn't even closed. Things had just gotten interesting.

As the realization sank in that I had a chance of having my own TV show, the first people I called were my grandparents, then my parents, then my brother. I thought, I have this wonderful opportunity—why wouldn't I share it with my family? Christopher was working more than sixty hours a week and Slade had a couple of weeks to give me, but then he had to leave for another job. I told my family, "We're doing this together. This is going to take off!"

My dad and my brother, Ryan, agreed to come to Minneapolis to be part of the show. They signed contracts with Magnetic, and Ryan brought my cousin along as an extra pair of hands. We jumped right in on restoring Lyndale, and straightaway some big problems became clear. In filming a TV show—as with restoring a house or building a business—the devil is in the details. You'll always be hurt worst by what you don't know.

The process was brand new to everyone involved. When you watch a home repair show on HGTV, everything looks organic. It's like the camera just happens to be there at the exact moment the plumber makes the crucial hookup, or while the carpenter finishes installing those new shelves. The host explains it as if everything happens without a hitch. But all that is a TV illusion, carefully crafted by professionals.

We were far from professionals. The truth was, Magnetic had never done a show like *Rehab Addict*. Along with *The Vanilla Ice Project*, it was the first docu-reality series for Scripps (owner of HGTV and DIY Network).

It was a new business and they were still straightening out the kinks in their own operation. We were filming willy-nilly. And I was lost—at one point I even agreed to hair and makeup after they said, "She looks scary on TV without makeup." For two episodes I looked like a bridesmaid from 1987 as opposed to myself. I quickly ended that. Anytime anyone was doing anything—installing a patch in an oak floor, taping new drywall, securing a sink to the wall—we'd film everything, with no idea of how it might be used to create episodes. We didn't even have a formal story editor or producer, which is the very first thing any TV show should have. So basically we just shot all day without an outline or direction, which was—in hindsight—insane. It would be like cooking everything you need to feed a family of thirty Thanksgiving dinner and then to realize that you only have one guest coming and they're vegan. Needless to say, much of the footage ended up on the cutting room floor.

The filming made the job site chaotic. Things quickly turned testy. My brother had left behind a girl he had just started dating in Detroit, the woman who would become his wife. So he was homesick from the minute he landed in Minneapolis. My house was packed with five guys and me, meaning nobody got much privacy or alone time. In addition to filming and renovating, I still had my real estate business, sometimes doing four open houses in a weekend. Everybody thought everybody else wasn't doing their fair share of work.

On top of everything, one of my allegedly "silent" partners wanted to tell us how everything should be done. When I was tiling a bathroom floor, he showed up with notebook and pencil in hand, pulled up a chair, and watched me work while he took notes. Then he researched tiling online or in some home-improvement book and came back with suggestions on how it should really be done. It was the worst kind of irritating. No surprise that tempers got mighty frayed before long.

Our family of four.

To make matters worse, money was short all around. People assume that when you have a show, you're raking in the cash. Our show was still being shot as a pilot, which meant there was no money being paid out. If the network liked it, they would order a whole season, which typically would be thirteen episodes. In the meantime, I was responsible for paying everyone and buying everything. In the six months it took to finish the Lyndale renovation, we cobbled together all of two and a half episodes. Not a great start. Oh, and you only get paid per episode—known as an episodic rate.

We had been working at Minnehaha around the clock, and it boiled down to about $2.25 an hour—I was right back to the days of my strawberry field wages. There was nothing to do when we finished Lyndale but wait and see if the network liked it. No one wanted to stick it out in Minneapolis.

My family headed home and Christopher and I finally called it quits.

The one good thing that came out of all that frustration was that the identity of the show became clearer. Of all the mistakes we had made starting out, one of the worst was that we didn't have a distinct vision. Was the show going to be about me and my family and crew, with everyone developing as a character? Were we going to play off interpersonal dramas? Once everybody left, it became clear that *Rehab Addict* should be about saving old houses, period. Those months spent filming the Lyndale house were a learning experience for everyone, and learning experiences are rarely pleasant.

Lyndale had become this huge, out-of-control project. Funny, because looking back, I now see it as a really simple project, especially given all the houses I've done on the show since. The good news was that the network liked what they saw and ordered a whole season—thirteen episodes. Magnetic hired a story producer and two shooters/producers. This was a huge deal for them as a new company and a big deal for me. There are not too many people in the world who get their own TV show. I knew I had to deliver if I wanted this to be sustainable. With a new film crew and a new plan in place, we all moved on to Minnehaha.

But after seeing what little money there was to be made, my family decided to stay in Detroit and not continue on with the show. I couldn't blame them. I was at least at home while filming and I had my real estate business to supplement my income. We moved forward. Ironically, Christopher stayed a contributing member of the "cast" because, like it or not, we still owned Minnehaha together.

John Kitchener had kept his word when he promised the next project would go smoother; he threw me a team composed of three experienced workaholic women just like me: Liz, Katie, and Christina. I watched and learned as they taught me how to outline episodes and story produce. The goal was to only shoot what we knew we wanted to put in the show. We had Post-it notes on a wall outlining the four major segments we'd need to cover for each episode. Once the segment was shot, down came the note. Lyndale had been an education in how a show like *Rehab Addict* works, how the episodes are formed. Minnehaha was where I put that learning to use.

But even with a good episode plan and being organized, there was no getting around the fact that Minnehaha would require a massive amount of labor. At the behest of Magnetic, I hired a general contractor. The contractor assured me he would get the work done on time, and for pennies. Most people assume that because my houses are on TV, all the work and materials are paid for. That's the furthest thing from the truth. Every dollar counts. Minnehaha, even for its horrible state, was not cheap. The renovation cost easily hundreds of thousands of dollars.

Christopher was forever complaining about how much money it was costing and how long it was taking, even though he was rarely on the job site. I'd say, "Get your ass to work then, and we won't have to have as many people on the payroll." Our relationship was anything but friendly at that point. Imagine Christina and Katie's surprise when they found Mr. White Collar wearing grubby clothes and staining the basement floor with me. My hope is always that once someone experiences the muscle burn of manual labor, they'll appreciate what hard work it is. This wasn't the case with Christopher, but like I said, I had hope. At one point, I had to finish painting the fireplace and Christopher was nowhere to be found, so everyone put down their cameras and there I was alongside Christina and Katie painting into the night.

As paint went on the walls in different rooms, the majestic character of Minnehaha really began to shine through. And we were wrapping episodes at a fast pace. The show was beginning to come together like a real TV show.

However, we were still months behind schedule. Even though the house wasn't finished, *Rehab Addict* premiered on October 14, 2010. The intent was that all thirteen episodes would be complete, but Minnehaha was so far from finished that HGTV aired five episodes and then put us on hiatus so we could complete the work.

During that hiatus, we scrambled to get the footage for the last eight episodes, and when I say scrambled, I mean we worked day and night. Minnehaha was our second home. And in those early episodes, you often see Ethan playing in the yard with his buddies. Ethan was still young enough that he and all of his friends wanted to be on TV. One of my favorite scenes was me having a snowball fight with Ethan. We were living and breathing *Rehab Addict*.

Recording voice-over for the first season.

Ethan was on always on-site at Minnehaha.

Once we had filmed the last episode on Minnehaha, the cameras went away, the work trucks drove off for the last time, and the house looked wonderful. Wonderful, but not even close to finished. The magic of filming a TV show is that you decide where the camera looks . . . and where it doesn't. In Minnehaha, as in every house featured on *Rehab Addict*, the project is never finished when the final episode wraps. I inevitably have a mile-long punch list of final details to complete before the house can be listed, much less sold.

There I was still working away on Minnehaha, now solo, when I got a call from Christina at Magnetic. "Hey, Nicole. We're ordering another season."

"Oh, good, great." I didn't really know what to say. I was exhausted. The good news was the show was a hit. People were identifying with my love for old houses. I wasn't surprised, but I'm pretty sure the network was. From the start of filming on the Lyndale house, my life had been like running downhill with scissors in my hand; I had just enough control, but not as much as I would have liked. After I finished the phone call, I was excited about the new season, but two things loomed over my head: Christopher had just moved out of the Yellow house and it was all mine but we were still at odds about what to do with

Minnehaha, and I also needed to find a house for *Rehab Addict*, season two. It was almost more than I could process.

But I took a deep breath and told myself that the more important thing to keep in mind was that Ethan was happy in Minneapolis. I was finishing up work on the house of my dreams, and I had a new career that, although I didn't know where it might go, was sure to lead somewhere exciting. All in all, there were more pluses than minuses.

I didn't set out to be on TV. It never really occurred to me. But I learned early on that opportunities are a gift. When they pop up, you don't hem and haw about whether it's the right thing at the right time. You don't worry about the work and frustration they will require. You certainly don't worry about all the things that could go wrong at any given point. Focusing on potential problems is a good way to freeze up and do nothing.

Christina, Katie, and me all painting the Minnehaha fireplace (left and center). The finished room (right).

No. You take advantage of opportunities. That means being a little fearless in going after them. If you always worry about how much you're risking, you'll forever say no to potentially wonderful adventures. I mean, despite all the tension, I don't regret falling in love and moving to Minneapolis or going on TV. Those were risks worth taking. Those risks are the price of admission to living a rich, full life. Most of all, I have no regrets about Minnehaha, my dream house. Even though that house has been like a stake through my heart, I loved it . . . but eventually I would have to learn to let it go.

*Chapter 3*

# THE THING WITH HAVING A BIG MOUTH IS THAT YOU HAVE TO BACK IT UP

## DOLLAR HOUSE

Imagine you discover your house is sitting on a bad foundation, a crumbling base full of top-to-bottom cracks and buckling surfaces. Now imagine that's the foundation of your life, that what you thought was certain and true was actually false. That love was hate, and that the plans you assumed were your future actually were an illusion. What a shock, right? Well, whether the problem lies with the house you've bought or the life you've made, the answer is the same: Start rebuilding at the bottom, where the problem is, or anything else you build will be doomed to collapse.

By the time I landed on the doorstep of a derelict home on Third Avenue in Minneapolis, my life was in worse shape than the house. The foundations

In the middle of filming season two.

of both were in ruins and needed to be replaced. I was basically faced with making good on all the things I'd said about myself. I learned from Steve when we lived in Tampa that I had to sell myself. That meant talking big. The thing about talking big is, you have to put big actions behind your words or nobody will take you seriously. The Dollar house would be where I proved the words I used to sell myself, where I backed up my big mouth and got myself on track.

For my second season of *Rehab Addict* in 2011, out of desperation, I had piecemealed together a whole season using my friend Ellen's bathroom, my friend Nick's kitchen, and the house of newlywed clients of mine—even two episodes on my own basement; we ended with the Harriet project. I had all my money tied up in Minnehaha and, quite frankly, couldn't fund another project for the show. Make no mistake: I had a #1 show on TV, but I still had to buy the houses I would renovate on camera. It's always been my money. And if I hadn't found projects to work on, the show could have easily ended right there. So hodgepodge it was.

There I was juggling many different projects, still running my real estate business and, most important, making sure I was home every day when Ethan finished school. I was content just being a mom and working. But everyone was pressuring me to date as it had been a long time since Christopher and I had broken up. As single moms know, in a world of married friends, you're always made out to be the odd duck. It didn't help that more often than not, Ethan would ask, "Why can't we just be like normal families?" It was killing me, because I would do anything for my child. In addition to all that, I found out he was being bullied in his new middle school and I saw my sweet, loving boy wear a sad face every day. It was crushing. I know some parents don't have a choice, and so I felt blessed to have options. I wasn't rich, but the show gave me extra income and I used it to find a better school for Ethan. I transferred him to a small Catholic school, similar to the one I had attended back in Michigan. There, all the teachers knew his name and treated him like their own child.

With Ethan thriving in his new school, work progressing, and the show doing well, I was feeling a little more confident. I thought, Why not try to go on some dates? However, it wasn't as simple as just trying online dating. The show was on the air and my face was becoming more recognizable. A friend of mine suggested a matchmaker. As soon as I heard that word, I burst into "Matchmaker, Matchmaker," that song from *Fiddler on the Roof*. But as I was to learn, my life was not a Broadway musical, and matchmakers don't guarantee happy endings, good endings, or even not-so-bad-but-doable endings.

Out for a walk in Minneapolis.

Matchmakers are one step above online dating. Unlike a dating website, a matchmaker vets your viable matches to weed out any potential disasters (well, at least in theory). This woman was a funny, spunky, high-energy chick. Even though she was younger than me, she made me feel like she was a big sister setting me up. The day after I sat down with her for our initial meeting, she called me. "Nicole, I have the perfect man for you."

I had my doubts, but the matchmaker assured me he was perfect. She described him and then added that he was a widower. I stopped her right there and said no. I didn't want anything messy and that just felt like trouble. Her words were "Please just meet him; I think this is it." She gave me contact information for a local businessman named Mark. She also gave him my number, and he called me at work. I already had butterflies in my stomach. I ended the call by suggesting we meet at the Minnehaha house. After two seasons of *Rehab Addict*, I was finding out how many creeps and weirdos there are in the world, and I wanted to be careful in case the guy turned out to be a potential stalker. I didn't want him knowing where I lived.

The first flowers I received from Mark.

When I pulled up to the curb, he was already standing on Minnehaha's porch, framed by the majestic stonework of the entryway. I immediately thought, Well, something is clearly wrong, because he looked way too perfect. He was hot like the type of dad you see among the other parents at school and think, How in the world does that happen? He was tall and in good shape. He had a meticulous hair-cut, and a natural "how *you* doin'?" smile that I'm sure got him just about anything he wanted. From my initial assessment it seemed like I would make it home alive, so we went out from there.

As we rode to dinner in his Jaguar convertible, I thought, This is too good to be true. I was giddy, which is not like me. But honestly, I hadn't been on a date in so long. I was either working with my hair tied up in a knot or running around looking like a mom with my hair tied up in knot. Now I actually had my hair down and my nails done, and I was wearing a dress. Things moved quickly. Within a week we had gone on three dates. One day I came home to find a beautiful flower arrangement in my living room. I thought, That's odd. How did these get in here? I asked Ethan, and he said he hadn't taken them in. I looked at the card, and they were from Mark, celebrating our first month together. I called him and casually asked how he'd gotten into the house. He said he'd gone around the back and found the door unlocked. I was a little more than weirded out, but then he showed up for dinner and treated me like a queen. Who cared if he'd come into my house uninvited? No big deal. Soon after that, we went kayaking and he forgot to bring a change of clothes. Boxes from Bloomingdale's and Nordstrom started to appear on my doorstep. He ordered a whole wardrobe to keep at my house so it wouldn't happen again.

I shrugged it off. I wasn't worried because he had told me everything I wanted to hear, especially that he wanted more kids. I loved being a mother, and having more children was what I wanted more than anything else. Mark also knew how to romance a gal. One Friday, on learning that Ethan was staying at a friend's house, Mark said, "Let's go away for the week-end." We booked a last-minute trip to Chicago and he told me to pack my dog, Polly (who traveled with me everywhere). He arranged to have Sade

Polly, in Chicago.

playing when we walked into our hotel room at the Trump Tower Chicago. He even fed Polly filet mignon. That moment meant so much, as Polly passed away a few weeks later. Remembering how he'd doted on my pup made me sure he was the one. When I came out dressed for dinner, he looked at me and said, "You're so beautiful." I had just spent three years in a relationship where the closest thing to a romantic exchange was "What a great price on that tile." The way Mark treated me felt good, and as much as I still had some hesitation, I did it: I just relaxed and let my guard down.

He opened car doors for me, and I would wake up to find a Starbucks venti green iced tea on the nightstand, with a yellow Post-it note saying, "I love you, baby." I had fought so hard and been on my own as a single mother for so long. The idea that this man treated Ethan like his son and said he was going to take care of us was really appealing. I also adored his daughter. I set up one of my guest bedrooms for her to use when she and Mark stayed over. The whole thing seemed ideal. I didn't realize that Mark was slowly but surely taking over. I had let my defenses down. Almost before I knew it, we became inseparable. My friends called us "the dream couple." It was easy to get sucked in. I've since asked those friends why they didn't let me know they thought something was up. They tell me that they saw me happy and didn't want to ruin it.

It turned out that there was darkness behind the curtain. Mark could be calm and nonchalant in public and high-strung and demanding in private. He hated hearing the word "no," and he wanted to be in charge, whether it was planning a vacation or choosing the restaurant for dinner. It's amazing, though, what you can ignore when you put your mind to it. I didn't raise a fuss when he developed the habit—anytime I questioned him or resisted something he said—of grabbing my chin between his forefinger and thumb, firmly holding my face in place, and staring into my eyes. He'd say, very slowly as if he were talking to a child, "You trust me, don't you? You love me? Let me handle it. I've got it." You get yourself into these situations bit by bit. You give yourself up a little at a time until you finally come to the point where you don't recognize the person in the mirror.

The Harriet house.

While the relationship with Mark grew more intense at lightning speed, dealing with the investors who had purchased the Harriet house could not have been more difficult. I had lost the house in a bidding war to them, and then had the genius idea of approaching them to let me work with them and use the house on my show. I loved the Harriet house and just wanted to make sure the original details were left intact. I had to get creative. The owners jumped at my offer to be on TV and to take advantage of the fact that it would garner exposure for their business.

A few days into filming, I realized I had made a mistake. My impatience had led me into another painful partnership. The house became a source of daily tension. The crew thought I was a prude because I wasn't cool with off-color humor on my set. My "partners" would show up un-announced and start berating me for my choice to save a claw-foot tub or for the tile color I'd picked. It got bizarre. I had to fight every inch of the way. If I wasn't being told what I was doing wrong, someone else was telling me how I could never do this alone.

The Harriet house was such a constant, over-the-top nightmare that I didn't even want to do a TV show anymore. I had put up with too much. I had listened to disparaging comments almost every day. One of the partners had actually said to me, after I negotiated a great price for some reclaimed cabinets, "It must be nice to be hot and blond."

Adding to my stress, Christopher had attempted to negotiate the sale of Minnehaha without conferring with me. I wanted to keep the house, but we couldn't agree on anything, so I had listed it. Unbeknownst to me, Christopher had been working with buyers.

At this point, I sat down with John Kitchener.

"I can't do this anymore, John," I told him.

"Nicole, come on."

"I can't, John. I just can't. I want to be home with my kids and taking care of Mark—not dealing with partners that don't respect me." At that time, Mark would arrive every day to have lunch with me. I didn't find out until later that someone had made a snide remark to him, implying that I had slept my way to the top. (I learned this months later in one of our final conversations.)

John had a knack for always cutting right to the chase. "Nicole, if you can just get through this, you're on the cusp of something huge. You have no idea how big this is going to be."

He was right, but it didn't matter. "I don't care, John. I'm done."

"Let's just say you're giving it some thought. Let's keep the door open."

Mark knew all this was happening. He assured me that I didn't need a TV show; I should just focus on him and the kids. One night, as we sat on my couch talking about Minnehaha, he grabbed my hands in his and looked me in the eyes. "I want to buy that house for you. I think you should always have it. It's where we met. I'm going to buy it for you and we'll live there."

Nobody had ever offered to take care of me that way. After pushing a rock uphill since forever, it was so seductive to just let someone else shoulder the burden. So I said, "Yes, let's buy the house. I'd love to live there."

In renovating old homes, I always tell people to take their time and do it right. Hastiness creates chaos. Yet I was ready to change everything after being with a guy for only six months. In my business life, I pump the brakes; I pay attention to details before making any moves. But in my personal life, one "I want to buy that house for you" was enough to make me throw caution to the wind. Within a matter of days, Mark had convinced Christopher to sell the house for less than it had been appraised for just for the sake of being done with it. When all the pieces came together, I couldn't believe it. It was like the clouds had parted and the sun was shining through; my dream life was within reach. But on the morning we were supposed to close, I looked over the paperwork and noticed that my name was nowhere to be seen. I held the papers out in front of Mark.

"Why's my name not on the contract?" I asked him.

"You can't worry about that right now."

"What do you mean I can't worry about it right now?"

"Look, we'll fix it later. But if we don't close today, we're not closing at all."

Mark was obsessed with anniversaries. We had met on the eleventh, and he wanted every important event in our lives to happen on the eleventh. The closing was scheduled for the eleventh, and it sounded to me like he was saying, "Close today or never." Alarms should have gone off. In hindsight, it should have been an easy call to delay the closing, but I wanted to ignore that sinking feeling in my gut and just trust him. Plus, it's not a huge deal to add a name to a deed after the fact. I've done it before (the other person just has to agree). The house represented a lot of hard work and, more important, the future. I could see in my mind's eye what it would be like living in that house. I knew exactly where the Christmas tree would go and how it would look all lit up on Christmas morning. I could imagine a baby crawling around on the maple floors while my dogs scuttled out of the way and kids cleared the table after a big family meal. I could see that new life so clearly that I didn't want to hold it up because of a mistake in the paperwork. So against my better judgment, I let the sale go forward.

After the closing, we drove from the lawyer's office straight to Minnehaha. We walked through the house, then upstairs. It seemed like a dream come true; after all the work, time, and frustration, the home of my dreams was mine. I walked into my master bedroom and stood there processing the reality, my eyes tearing up. Mark stood at the door, smiling at me.

"It's yours, baby. There's no more trouble. I just want you to soak it in. Because it's never going to get taken away from you again."

For the first time in a very, very long time, I felt totally safe, secure, and free. But when things seem too good to be true, they usually are. As we navigated two busy lives with two kids, two dogs, and three houses, I regularly brought up the issue of Minnehaha's paperwork.

"When are we going to do the paperwork to get my name on the deed?"

Mark would grab my chin, stare into my eyes, and say, "Do you trust me? Do you love me?" Then, "You need to stop worrying about this. Listen to me, Nicole Curtis. There are no worries here. I'm here to take care of you. Go buy some furniture."

So I went out and bought furniture—lots of it. I shopped for weeks, finding just the right pieces. The day finally came to move my piano, which had originally been in my grandparents' house, into the sunroom at Minnehaha. I remember sitting there thinking how amazing my life was, seeing my family's piano, with "Grinnell Brothers, Detroit" stamped on it, in my Minnehaha house.

I was ready to move when Mark dropped a bomb on me. We were discussing when we would move into Minnehaha, and what the future looked like, when he said, "I'm not having any more children. I'm absolutely not having any more children. I don't want any more."

"Wait a second," I told him. "You said you wanted more children. You knew I wanted more children when we met. I told the matchmaker that was a priority. We have to discuss it."

Ethan playing the family piano that has moved to each house with us.

The master bedroom in the Minnehaha house, before (left) and after (right).

He grabbed my chin, looked into my eyes, and said, "Do you love me? Do you trust me? We have two children and that's enough." And that was the end of the discussion as far as he was concerned. The truth is, had I known he didn't want more children, I would never have met with him. It was a deal breaker for me and something I had been up front about when I first met the matchmaker.

But all the chin grabbing in the world wasn't going to settle the subject for me. I felt like Mark had misled me. I needed a little space and time to think things through. I wasn't going to be able to properly process everything with someone holding on to my chin. I told him I needed a break and that we'd talk when I'd had a chance to figure some things out. I didn't make any threats and I didn't say I was breaking up with him. But he was clearly unhappy with the idea.

I called my closest girlfriends and used them as sounding boards. They were all supportive. But in the end, I realized that no one else could give me the answer. I searched my soul and eventually came to a conclusion. The way I figured it, God doesn't give you everything you ask for. That's not how it works. I asked for another child, and God brought me this little girl who had lost her mom. I realized that she needed me more than I needed a baby.

A few days after I told Mark I was "taking a break," he wouldn't answer my phone calls. I had just arrived home and was chatting with my plumber, who had been doing some work, when Mark burst through the front door. He had written me a fifteen-page letter and he threw it onto the coffee table.

"You want this to be over? Fine, it's done. You're done. I'm done."

"Whoa! Calm down," I told him. I was horrified that he had exploded like this.

"I *am* calm, Nicole. You need to understand what you did."

He was so worked up. I grabbed my coat and pushed him out the door. We drove to Minnehaha, where I thought that at the very least, he could "air" his frustration without an audience. The minute we walked in the door, I went up to the master bedroom; it was the place where he'd told me on the fateful January 11 that the house was mine. I hoped that room would bring some peace. I had just finished placing all the furniture, and I walked over to the west end of my beautiful dressing room and asked him to sit. He had gotten himself into such a state that it didn't seem like anything was going to calm him down.

"You left me? You're done, Nicole. I'm done."

"I just needed some time to think; I didn't say I didn't love you," I told him. "Before I even met you, I said that I wanted more children. I wanted to share that with whomever I met. But you haven't even given me a chance to tell you what I think." I proceeded to explain my thoughts to him and said that we could make it work. I thought he would be overjoyed, but for a man who cried at the drop of a hat, he had no tears. Just a look of disdain.

I told myself, You go through rough patches. That's how real-life relationships work. You get through them and the relationship is stronger for it. In the weeks that followed, I plowed ahead. Every week I would move another piece of furniture, another chair or side table, into Minnehaha. I brought in dishes and lamps and everything we'd need to be a real family under one roof. That was still the plan. One big happy family. But when I tried to pin Mark down and set a move-in date, I was in for a surprise.

I said, "We should really start looking at schools."

"We can't do that right now."

"What do you mean?"

"My daughter doesn't want to move and leave her friends; it's breaking her heart."

"Okay, well, what's the plan? What are we doing?"

"I have to think about it and let you know." If I pushed, it turned into an argument. Moving into Minnehaha had been his idea. I simply wanted to be together. He had told me that everyone was excited about Minnehaha. It was going to be a good move for his little girl, because a lot of her friends lived nearby and it would mean a fresh start for everyone. His daughter meant the world to me, and I was shocked by what he was saying now—as if I would want to see her sad or hurting. And truly, if this wasn't going to work, then I just wanted to figure out what would, but he wouldn't have it. In Mark's life, he was always the boss.

He and I still went to Minnehaha almost every day. We'd grab some takeout Chinese, sit at the island in the kitchen, and relax. Even after a couple of glasses of wine, Mark didn't want to talk about anything that would commit him to action. I had moved most of what I could into Minnehaha. I was ready. But we were in limbo when he scheduled a trip for us to Palm Springs, to spend Easter with his parents. I thought it might be a nice get-away, out of chilly Minneapolis to someplace where we could soak up some of that nice desert sun. It seemed like a low-key family vacation would give us a good opportunity to discuss moving forward. It turned out to be any-thing but low key.

Mark didn't want to stay with his parents. We stayed at a golf resort. I had figured out that I shouldn't ask questions, so I just went with it. With his family, I never knew what was the right thing to do. When we started dating, I had met his parents. His mom had helped him orchestrate an over-the-top birthday celebration for me. I thought they were lovely people, so I followed their lead and included them in the dinners and events that I had. It was only later that someone revealed to me that prior to dating me, Mark had not made his parents very welcome in his life. With the trip to Palm Springs, I didn't know what to think.

On Saturday morning, his mom took his daughter shopping; the boys went golfing. I asked if I should join the girls and was surprised when Mark suggested I take the day for myself. He assured me it was okay, saying, "Baby, enjoy the sun, relax." I started by going to the gym and realized I hadn't packed any socks. Never one to give up, I ended up wearing youth hockey socks. (For whatever reason, the resort had a pair of those for sale.) I sent Mark a picture and he texted back, "That's my girl; I love you. Can't wait to see you."

Later that day, refreshed from a day on my own, I called up an artist I had met online, the incredible Elizabeth Lyons. We had bonded over e-mail in recent months and I wanted to meet her in person. I asked her to come to the hotel and have a drink. She had just arrived and we were sitting down

The hockey sock picture I sent Mark (top). Me and Elizabeth having some girl time (bottom).

enjoying a glass of wine when Mark came back from golfing. My mood was great; I had just been telling Elizabeth about the fairy tale that my life was becoming. As Mark headed toward me, my stomach turned; I could see that something was wrong. I introduced Elizabeth, and he said hi and that he was going up to the room to change. I confided in Elizabeth that I felt my life was too good to be true. I had never had the luxury of spending a day by myself at a resort, then having a glass of wine with a girlfriend, and it felt very glamorous. Did I finally have the life my married girlfriends had bragged about? If this was it, I was in!

I have a picture of me and Elizabeth from that day. I look confident and happy. I had no idea that when I went upstairs, my life was going to implode. Mark was agitated. I asked him what was wrong, which apparently was not the right thing to say at that moment. From there it went from bad to ugly to me spending the entire night begging for forgiveness. For what? For choosing to spend a day by myself. *Really.*

He had set me up. Mark didn't want me to have a relaxing day; he wanted me waiting for him. And poor Elizabeth was the last straw. How dare I be so comfortable as to invite a friend over on our vacation? The night went on and on; I felt ashamed. I was exhausted. The kids had gone to the movies with his parents and I was stuck with him. I had had enough. I asked the fateful question: "When are you going to tell your parents that we're moving in together?"

"We're not. Actually, Nicole, we're done."

"What?"

"It's over. I'm not doing this anymore."

It kept going like this late into the night. Everything I thought was true was a lie. He knew what I was looking for from the matchmaker, and he had offered it all, knowing deep down that if he had told the truth, I would have never met with him. At the end, he seemed to snap back to reality and said, "I love you; I'm sorry."

We woke up in the morning, and the next thing I knew, I was sitting in a church pew next to him, the kids, and his parents. Like nothing had happened. That was the start of what was easily the most awkward holiday dinner I've ever attended. It was followed by an equally awkward flight home. I thought, If this is over, I'll deal with it as I do everything else. But just ending it wouldn't be good enough for Mark.

I would ask him, "What are we doing?" and he would blow me off. And if I pressed more, he'd get angry. I was done playing his games and walking on eggshells. I started to do what I could to get my ducks in a row. It brought me peace to check on the house every day and reassure myself that it was still there and he hadn't magically made it disappear.

Minnehaha became my sanctuary. It seemed like things had gone so wrong so quickly that it was astounding. In a short time, I had gone from planning my dream life in my dream house with my dream man to dealing with a life in shambles.

I arrived one spring day to do my usual check on the house and enjoy an hour or two of solitude before I had to pick up Ethan, only to find that my key didn't work. My key to the house that I had bought and restored long before Mark had ever set foot on my front porch didn't work.

Things got ugly. Like Lifetime movie ugly. I didn't know what to do. To make matters worse, a number of my friends told me that Mark was spreading rumors that I was mentally unstable. I was at a complete loss, and being the type of person who always has to fix everything, I decided that if there *was* something wrong with me, I would get to the bottom of it. I called another mom from Ethan's school who was a doctor. Not just any doctor, a neuropsychologist.

I told her, "Mark says I have borderline personality disorder. Be honest with me. Do I? Am I that screwed up?"

And this woman saved my life.

"Oh my god, Nicole," she said. "No. No. No. I am going to refer you to someone. You go see this doctor."

I had done therapy in my teens and in my twenties, every few years to get a tune-up. Wise people know that a mental health counselor is to your brain what a personal trainer is to your body. Unfortunately, mental health is so misunderstood that some people think you have to be crazy to need to speak to a therapist. Think about it: The majority of the people I know who use trainers are my fittest of friends; they're triathletes and competitive runners. It's the same with my friends who get counseling to get in their best mental shape. There is always room for improvement. This is how I view therapy.

I was reassured by the doctor that I didn't have borderline personality disorder. Anxiety? Yeah. Issues with self-confidence? Yeah. Bad taste in boyfriends? Definitely. But most of all, I was broken and sad, which is a natural reaction to such a traumatic breakup. I was empowered to start to rebuild.

The very next day, I went to work making good on a chance meeting I'd had while I was rebuilding the Harriet house. I had been out in front of the house, cleaning up the walkway to the front door, when a guy pulled up to the curb and got out of his car. Brian Finstad looked like the poster boy for Northern Minnesota. A stocky young man with a friendly round face and a beard, he wore glasses that made him look scholarly and a flannel shirt that made him look a model in an L.L. Bean catalog.

"You're Nicole Curtis!"

"Yes, I am."

"There's a house down the street you need to save."

My first day at the Dollar house.

It turned out that he was a local preservationist and had once owned a house in the Central neighborhood, where this house was. He couldn't have been nicer, and we talked about the house for a few minutes. After I was certain he wasn't an ax murderer, I got into his car and drove with him down Third Avenue, to the sad little structure that would become known to *Rehab Addict* viewers as the Dollar house. It was a dingy, boarded-up place, with a mud-brown-and-beige color scheme that just made it seem dingier. Someone had painted the address on a board over the front door. But otherwise, there wasn't any indication that the house had been touched in a decade.

It was ironic. As soon as we drove up, I realized I had tried to buy the house two years before. The parties couldn't agree on a price that satisfied everyone, so I had walked away. And here it was, a couple of years later, and they literally couldn't give the house away. The city had condemned it and recommended it for demolition.

The Dollar house exterior, before (left), during (center), and after (right) renovations.

Brian and I slowly walked around the boarded-up, corner-lot 1911 bungalow. The yard was overgrown and scraggly. There were large sections of stucco missing from the sides of the house. Still, I could tell that it had lots of potential even before we unscrewed the board covering the front door. The good news was that it was still standing and there was actually a lot of great woodwork left inside. But there was one big problem—the foundation. I kicked a basement wall with my boot and it went through about six inches. That's never a good sign. But it wasn't the end-all, as I had dealt with foundation issues before. The question was, was it repairable? And could I get a structural engineer to tell me how it could be fixed?

"Look, Brian, I'm swamped," I told him. "I think the house is totally worth saving, but I just don't have the time and patience to deal with the red tape. But if you can get the paperwork through the city, I'll rehab it."

I give Brian credit. He rallied some of the neighbors and other community activists to petition the city and cut through the bureaucracy at Minneapolis' Community Planning and Economic Development (CPED) department. The city agreed to rescind the property demolition order so the house could be sold to me and the work could begin. However, I was under no illusions. CPED had the project on a short leash. One slipup and they would swoop in and demolish the house.

At that point, Minneapolis was fighting blight, and the easy solution was to tear down dilapidated houses. The theory was, better a vacant lot than a boarded-up wreck. I didn't understand that way of thinking, but that was the majority vote. What most people didn't understand is that a lot like the one the Dollar house sat on was no longer a legal-size lot, according to the standards of city planners. Therefore, if the house were torn down, nothing, and I mean nothing, could ever be built there again.

The nonprofit that owned the house simply wanted it off their books. Understandably; so would I. Now I offered them a solution. Brian worked with them and we finally got the title transferred to me. In real estate, even a free house needs a value. The minimum? One dollar. Thus 3049 Third Avenue became the Dollar house. Because most of my ready cash was still tied up in Minnehaha, the low purchase price offered a rare opportunity I could take advantage of. And the project would be all mine, so it was also a way to silence my critics, those doubters who kept telling me I couldn't rehab a house by myself. I saw the Dollar house as a way to back up everything I had said I could do all along.

With my plans for a future as a stay-at-home mom pretty much destroyed, I decided I needed to get back in the game and keep my career alive. I called John Kitchener and told him that not only was I in for another season of *Rehab Addict*, but that I'd also found a house ready to go for the next season. He scheduled a film crew. I went to work putting the word out that we were going to save this house. We scheduled a pre-renovation open house, something I was doing for the first time. Oddly enough, Mark insisted on attending! He said, "I'm here to support you." What?! I didn't know what to think. I just went with it. My friend Lauren took what would be the final picture of Mark and me together on the stairs that day.

I had great support from the neighbors of the Dollar house.

People lined up for hours to see the "before" of this project. Everyone asked, "Why would you show the house before it's done?" Here's why: I wanted every single person I could cram in to see what terrible shape this house was in. I wanted the smell of abandonment to sneak up their noses and the hazards of vacant houses to be within reach of each person's own fingertips. It was a simple marketing idea. If they could see how bad the house was when they walked through it the first time, when we were finished, they would see with their own eyes that any house—no matter how dilapidated—can be saved. The Dollar house would be my proof.

@NCRehabAddict I'm moving the minnehaha house right now.

Tweetbot for iOS · 5/23/12 7:56 AM

The tweet.

After the open house, Mark looked at me and said, "You know, I'm selling the house." I looked at him in shock. The next few weeks would be even more confusing with no more mentions of selling the house. Until someone tweeted me about it. Apparently, without further discussion, he had made arrangements to put the house up for sale. I arrived at Minnehaha to find an off-duty Minneapolis cop standing guard on the porch.

"You're going to have to leave, ma'am."

"Leave? This is my house." I tried calling Mark, but he wouldn't pick up. I looked inside and saw his mom packing boxes.

I shouted through the window, "What's going on? Someone needs to come out here and tell me what's going on."

She came out onto the porch, flustered and looking guilty. "You need to leave, Nicole. I was told to box everything up and take it to a storage unit, or we can take it to wherever you want. But you can't be here." I stood there dumbfounded. The movers, his mother, and his assistant were going through my house, and my things, and throwing them all into boxes. Months later, when I finally found the courage to unpack those boxes, I came across one that was labeled "Dirty Dishes from Dishwasher." That was an all-new low for me.

My Gramps had always made me promise that I would be a smart businesswoman. There is not a chance in hell that I would ever give up my stake in Minnehaha. Even for love. I e-mailed Mark a purchase agreement for Minnehaha. He agreed to sell it to me for what he had bought it for. I was over the moon. A few days later, on our one-year anniversary, June 11, Mark sent me a message saying I should go to the Minnehaha house; he had left something for me there. On the steps were a dozen roses. I'm sure had I swooned and been

The roses.

sucked in, the keys to that house would be on my key chain right now. But I'm my grandmother's granddaughter, and I didn't need some man turning my head. I took the flowers and broke them into little pieces and threw them on the porch. The next day, I got a call from Mark's attorney; the price to buy my own house had gone up fifteen thousand dollars. I said okay. Then the price went up fifteen thousand dollars more. I still said okay, but I was sick to my stomach. Unfortunately, things went further south from there. Right before we were about to close, I got a call from Bridgewater Bank, saying that they had heard from an unknown source that I wasn't a good investment for their bank and they had canceled my mortgage. I immediately sent Mark an extension to the purchase agreement, a common practice in real estate, and he refused it.

I had to make a decision: let the house go or sue Mark for it. This would change the way I do business for the rest of my life. I felt ashamed that I had let "love" blind my business mind. I retained an attorney and filed suit shortly thereafter. It would take years for the litigation to wind through the courts. All that money wasted. And my house sat there. After all these years, when I reflect on putting up a fight for that house, do I regret it? Absolutely not.

The lawsuit would ultimately drain my savings and rob me of years of peace. The house would be in legal limbo for years as the case dragged on—all the way to the Minnesota Court of Appeals. At the end of the day, Mark got the house, and I learned a lesson. Some people will say and do anything to make a wrongdoing seem right.

It was June of 2012, and I focused on moving forward. I pulled up my bootstraps and got to work on the Dollar house.

From the very start, we had a lot of local support on that house. The neighbors were tired of watching druggies pull down the boards covering the doors so that they could sneak inside and use the house as a shooting gallery. I had made a promise to the city and the neighborhood from the get-go: "If you turn that house over to me, I'll clean it up, not destroy it. I'm going to put a new owner in that house. And nothing is better for neighborhood revitalization than an owner-occupant. Neighborhoods need people with a stake in the future if they are going to come back and thrive."

Words can be powerful, but you have to back them up. I was faced with rebuilding the house with virtually no budget and few resources. As with the rest of my life at that point, it was going to mean starting from the ground up.

I hired a structural engineer to assess the foundation. I held my breath, hoping that he would say it could be reinforced and repaired. It would have been great if we could have done a little shoring-up work in the basement, spending a few thousand dollars at most, and had a solid base for the house. But I had worked with enough bad foundations to know it probably wasn't going to be that simple. In the end, the engineer took my check and left me with a report that came to a no-doubt conclusion: The foundation had to be completely replaced. Replacing an existing foundation means lifting the entire house, something very few contractors ever have to do. But lucky me, I was about to become one of the select few.

If you're going to do something as challenging and tricky as raising a whole house, replacing the foundation, and then putting the house back in place, you better have the best people working for you. That meant contractor after contractor would have to be interviewed in order to find someone who could do the job right and work for an amount I could actually pay. And this is where Leif came in. Leif is the brother of one of my clients. He had had the unfortunate task of helping me deal with all the boxes that came out of Minnehaha, and now he needed some work. More important, Leif had the time and the patience to meet the contractors at the house and let them in to inspect everything, again and again. (Incidentally, the sound of an impact drill taking out boarding bits is one that I can recognize from a million miles away. There are no doorknobs on abandoned houses—simply boards held in with special screws, and you need a "boarding bit" to get them out. You know a house preservationist when you see boarding bits in the cup holders of his or her car!)

We ended up interviewing almost twenty contractors before we found one who had the right credentials and experience, and could stay within my budget. Still, the job would cost me thirty thousand dollars, which was all the money I had on hand for the Dollar house.

One of the wonderful things about rehabbing decrepit buildings is that you're always learning something new. I'd never lifted a house. First things first: We had to remove the chimney. I also used the opportunity to conquer my fear of heights when I climbed a ladder to the top of the roof to dismantle the compromised chimney. This sounds easy enough, but when you need to take down a chimney, whatever you think will be required is probably wrong. You have to climb to the top of the roof, and then to the top of the chimney, which is a good three to four feet higher than your roof peak. You then sit there and start to chisel it away brick by brick. And where do the bricks go? Into a bucket that you have to continuously lower to the ground to get emptied.

Filming at the Dollar house happened around the clock.

Look at any chimney; they're made of a lot of bricks. We started on that chimney early in the morning and it took us till early evening to finish removing all the bricks. The best part for me was that with every brick I removed, it put me closer to the ground.

While I was working on the house, Ethan was enjoying the first few days of summer vacation, coming over to the job site for fun—definitely not to work. I loved when he showed up. There's a scene in one early Dollar house episode where Ethan chases me through the house and touches my face with his dirty hands to make me scream, because he knows I'm a germophobe. Moments like these play over and over in my mind; the pure joy of horseplay and nonsense that comes with raising boys. He still liked the show back then and loved scheming with the crew to play pranks on me. Everyone loved to goof around.

My lead cameraman was Eric Klang. As far as camera operators go, many of them are twenty- or thirty-somethings, a few are in their forties, and then there is Eric. No offense to Klang, but the gray hair always made people assume he was more likely to be reading a book in the shade than jumping over walls, two-by-fours, shovels—you name it—to grab the shot. Not only is Klang a would-be gymnast, but he has, without a doubt, the most profound talent of telling you BS with a straight face, so you couldn't tell fact from fiction. I arrived one day to the job site and said, "Morning, Klang. Any news?"

"Nothing much. Just kicked a prostitute and her customer off the steps when I arrived."

And then without skipping a beat, he went on to tell me which shots he had gotten and where we were in the filming. To say that that part of Minneapolis was still very dicey was the understatement of the year. I was never surprised at what Klang would report, but if I looked worried, Klang

Ethan heading to Michigan with Max.

would just matter-of-factly say, "Well, that's what comes with what you do." Don't get me wrong; Klang and I have had our share of differences of opinion over the years, but it was at the Dollar house that he gave me some great advice one day when we were getting ready to film.

"Nicole, just remember that this might be an ordinary day for you, but when you are shooting with people who don't do this regularly, it might be the coolest day of their lives."

It's reminders like this that have kept me grounded over the years. And after that, I thought that what Klang said is exactly right. Why not give this TV opportunity to everyone to enjoy? So I made an unprecedented move: I opened my construction site to visitors. After signing a release promising not to hold me liable, anyone who wanted to be a part of the action could visit, help out, and hang out at the Dollar house. Jose, our newly appointed production assistant from Chicago, was in charge of the "fans."

Jose is an imposing six feet plus with a shaved head, and within two seconds of meeting you, he'll let you know that he's Puerto Rican. This description makes him sound like he could be a security guy, and over the years he has become exactly that and more, but at the Dollar house he was Klang's right-hand man.

The day to raise the house came, and it was a fascinating process separating the house from the foundation. I even drove a Bobcat through the basement wall. We lifted the house and within three days set it back down.

That's when the volunteers came in droves. Jose would welcome them with a smile and a release form. He'd call out to me, "Ma, we got a group from Pittsburgh. Ma, these folks drove from Chicago."

Amazingly, people were driving and flying in from all over the country to come see us at work. I would stop what I was doing, climb down from the ladder, pose for a picture, and go right back to work.

Some folks came by for an hour. Others worked for almost the entire project. Every day brought new faces, new, funny situations, and progress on the house. Ethan left for Mackinac Island with my parents, so my only responsibility was getting the Dollar house done and filmed. My friend Justin came from Michigan to help me. There we were: me, Klang, Leif,

Me, Jose, and Klang.

Jose, and Justin. It was mayhem and I loved it. I had lived in a bubble of negativity for the past few years, and I was coming back to being me.

We were on the job site around the clock. I started shooting small videos to post on Facebook. It really was uplifting to find fun in renovation again. On any given night, a friend would call and say, "I'm coming by with Chinese food and beer." We'd sit around out front, laughing and eating. Then I'd get back to work. I'd work all day, and then at ten at night, I'd wind up painting rooms or power washing the house. The neighbors never complained. They were so excited to see us turning a longtime trouble spot into a family home, we could do no wrong.

When we were ready to paint the interior, I did a callout for a paint day to get some help, and thirty people showed up. Many folks took a vacation day from work—yes, a vacation day—to be there. I was in awe and humbled at the same time. One regular group of painters became known as "the Ladies That Paint." Every day until we were done, they would come after work with paint clothes in hand and paint into the wee hours of the night. And around this time, a mystery man who had been chasing me started coming by and helping us out (hint: Chad). After a little landscaping, the house had incredible curb appeal. My punishing schedule of long days and longer nights was being rewarded with a beautiful house that would help transform a neighborhood— and prove that I could do what I had always said I could. All that working left me little time to ponder what might have been, with Mark or anyone else. As the summer came to a close and we wrapped

Justin and me rebuilding the porch.

up filming on the house, I felt like I was a new me. Or maybe I had rediscovered the old me, the me that could do anything I set my mind to.

The Dollar house was one of the rare projects that I was sorry to see come to completion. But the final product was well worth all the effort and the craziness. The house had a new foundation that would keep it standing for another hundred years and a historically accurate look. I could not have been prouder of the house, the people who helped make it a reality, and the neighborhood that supported our efforts.

Some of "the Ladies That Paint."

Even though I often felt like I was working at odds with the city itself, I had one of my most satisfying moments in the Dollar house when Elfric Porte, the manager of residential and real estate development for CPED, called me one day. Porte was always a straight shooter with me, and one of the best people I ever dealt with in the city bureaucracy.

"Nicole, I'd love to see the inside of that house you just finished."

"Sure. I'll meet you over there."

We walked through the house together and he stopped and admired the fireplace, and spent a long time looking at the redone bathroom with its stunning period mosaic floor tile. Elfric is not a big talker. But when we walked back out onto the new porch, looking over the tidy front-yard landscaping, he nodded.

The Dollar house living room, before (left) and after (right).

"You did a really great job on that, Nicole. It's beautiful."

I'd gotten my mojo back and established my credibility to anyone who might have doubted my words. The Dollar house was my statement—of who I was, what I was looking to achieve with *Rehab Addict*, and what I was capable of accomplishing. I'd managed to build a brand-new foundation not only for a historic house, but for my life as well. Sometimes you have to put actions behind your words, even when that means starting all the way at the bottom and building back up from scratch. The foundations I'd re-created for the Dollar house and for my life were going to serve me well, proof in the future that I would do anything I said I would.

# Chapter 4

# OWN THE PROCESS OR THE PROCESS WILL OWN YOU

## CASE AVENUE HOUSE

Although the Dollar house should have completed season three of *Rehab Addict,* it was only seven episodes, which meant I was short five episodes. Once again, I had to find a house to shoot. The houses in my life always overlap. You can't really tell the story of one house without touching on the story of another. That was the way it was with Case Avenue, purchased shortly after we began work on the Summit mansion, a new project.

The Summit mansion was monstrous. I mean, it's a mansion; it's over eight thousand square feet. The network wanted those final five episodes, and they couldn't get them fast enough. We couldn't delay our delivery, and I knew the work on that big house was going to take at least one to two years.

The Case Avenue house exterior, before (top) and after (bottom) renovations.

So I had to find a stopgap house. That was when the Case house opportunity came my way.

At this point, would I jump ship from one project to the next just for the sake of more episodes? Heck, no. It's a disaster. But I didn't have the wisdom of experience then, and Lord knew I couldn't afford to risk the network losing interest. In other words, I had no choice but to strike while the iron was hot.

My e-mail in-box is constantly flooded with messages about foreclosed properties and estate sales. A lot of these come from what I call real estate "carpetbaggers." These are a special kind of vulture that preys on people who are overextended in their homes and/or financially vulnerable through divorce, a death in the family—you name it, they exploit it. They swoop in, offer the family a minimal amount of money for the house, and then turn around and sell it to outside investors for a huge, quick profit.

These kind of investors aren't worried about anyone but themselves. They just want to turn a fast buck. Case was typical. It was a cute little 1890s house—well, my version of cute—in the Payne-Phalen neighborhood of

St. Paul. Just like the owner of the 20K house, this elderly owner had moved on to a nursing home. It was in utter disrepair, and I'm sure this was why the family had decided to sell it. Unfortunately, the only path they found was one of these carpetbagger investors, who, I would find out later, quickly scooped up the place for the paltry sum of less than ten thousand dollars. That person then sent information about the house in an e-mail blast to investors. I was one of them, and I was intrigued. I didn't know this neighborhood, but I'd become a victim of my own success. The Minneapolis neighborhoods where I had already rehabbed houses had bounced back just as they were supposed to. But that rebound jacked up prices even on fixer-uppers in those neighborhoods. I wasn't going to make it work financially anywhere close to home, which meant heading into St. Paul.

The estate houses I buy—like the 20K house and the Case house—can be risky in surprising ways. Not only am I paying for a house that may need much more work than is feasible given the budget, but I'm also inserting myself into an emotionally charged family situation. More than once, I've had someone contact me and say that I was profiting from their misery. It's especially common when family members see the house after I'm finished with it. Not having been there throughout the process, they assume it just came together like magic. They forget what it looked like, the condition it was in when I bought it, and how much money I'd had to put into it.

That's why, long ago, I decided to make the previous owners an offer on every house I rehab. If the original owner or a family member wants to buy the house back after I'm done, I'll sell it to them for my cost.

I was at Summit and discussing the situation with Chad. He was completely supportive of the idea of my switching to the Case house and even took it one step further, floating me the twenty-seven thousand dollars to buy it. I listed the Dollar house at the end of September 2012, and it was sold within three days. However, as real estate goes, the time between offer to closing is typically thirty to sixty days. Therefore, when I was ready to purchase Case, I didn't yet have the proceeds from the sale of the Dollar house. Although it was risky to buy one house when I hadn't sold the other, I was confident the Dollar house sale would go through, and I didn't really have a choice; I needed to get on with season three.

I truly thought Case would take no more than a few months to do, so I wasn't worried about it causing delays at the Summit mansion. After all, we'd had to *lift* the Dollar house and completely rebuild it, and that only took from May to October. But what I wasn't taking into account was that Case would be an entirely different project. I hadn't stopped to think what effect a Minneapolis winter would have on productivity. We'd completed the Dollar house over a summer, working almost nonstop. But how do you paint a house in single-digit weather? Or repair a porch? What do you do when the daylight just disappears on you after a few hours of work?

Even getting started on Case was an adventure. At the walk-through before the closing, I discovered it hadn't been cleaned out. Oftentimes, when someone sells a house under stressful conditions and for very little money—especially when an elderly relative has lived there—they just abandon the house and everything in it. The family of the woman who owned Case didn't want to plow through decades' and decades' worth of belongings. I suppose there's a sense of sadness or defeat that people want to get beyond as quickly as possible.

I had the romantic notion that I could rehab the belongings that were left in the house the same way I rehabbed houses. Clean and mend clothes and take them to a thrift shop. Fix and refinish furniture. Clean up antique picture frames and salvage them. I've since learned through tough experience that renovating a house is hard enough. Trying to bring someone else's belongings back to life is a fool's errand. Leif and I spent hours sorting through stuff. And amazingly, much of everything you see staged in Case was there when we got it.

There was also a deceptively large amount of work that needed to be done. Reporters who interviewed me and profiled Case would later say that what we did to the house were "cosmetic repairs," and in a sense they were right. There wasn't any serious structural damage. But the cosmetic damage was the most extreme I had ever seen. The water damage alone

Adam and me, working late into the night.

was appalling. Wood floors were warped throughout the house. Most of the walls had severe cracks and ugly black-and-gray water stains. The furnace needed to be replaced. The mouse infestation had, at one time, been so bad that mice had worn a track in the carpeting all around the perimeter of a room. I could have just torn everything out, but I wanted to save the exquisite wood moldings and woodwork throughout the house. It's what gave Case most of its charm. Each of these problems, taken on its own, wasn't especially troublesome. But add all of them together and I was facing a lot more work than I had anticipated.

I also underestimated what working in St. Paul would mean. I was so used to commuting just a few minutes to a job site—on Dollar, I'd often ridden to the house on my Vespa—that I was shocked to see how much the forty-minute commute to Case ate into my daily schedule. Just when I'd get into the middle of tearing out some stinky, ruined mess, I'd have to knock off to be home for Ethan. By the time I made it back to the house, it would be pitch black and freezing cold.

The actual work was, fortunately, straightforward. The floors in almost every room had buckled so badly that individual oak strips were "tented" and had to be cut out and replaced. We began painting the outside

The Case Avenue house dining room, before (top) and after (bottom).

of the house, but then it started snowing, so we switched gears and worked room by room, repairing plaster walls, and—my favorite—stripping woodwork. (In this episode, I referenced one of my best tricks: stripper in a can. Which led me to discover the sophomoric attitude of my viewers. There is now no end to stripper-in-a-can references.) Then there was the kitchen.

Kitchens are always challenges in the homes I rehab. Although I prefer to stick with original features as much as possible, renovating an old kitchen means installing updated technology and improved materials where necessary. I have to balance historical authenticity with the need for a modern, functional room. And I have to weigh both of those considerations against the budget. The Case kitchen had one set of old cabinets that I wanted to reuse, but I needed to integrate them with other cabinets—without paying for custom cabinetry that would break the bank. I split the difference by installing shelves in areas that would normally feature cabinets. Keeping that kitchen's look while modernizing its function took every bit of energy and creativity I had.

Much as I can be surprised by what a house hides once I start renovating it, there's usually little I haven't dealt with before. The real wild cards are always the neighbors. What I do is as much about the neighborhood as it is about the house, so the neighbors always figure into any of my projects. (They also affect how the house will sell after I'm done.) Where the neighbors were concerned, Case was an example of extremes. On one side lived a Hmong immigrant family who had a flock of chickens in their backyard. I didn't think much of it until one afternoon Leif came rushing into the house, eyes wide open in shock.

"You're not going to believe what's going on next door."

"What?"

"You just have to see it for yourself."

The Case Avenue house staircase, before (left) and after (right),
and those incredible stained glass windows.

Leif led me out the back door and we stood there watching as an older
Hmong woman caught and butchered chickens. Blood, guts, and feathers
were flying everywhere. When she was through, there were dead chickens
all over the backyard. It was quite the sight, and not really what you hope
for when you're anticipating putting a house on the market.

On the other side, though, lived Jerry. Jerry was a wonderful, sweet
man who took meticulous care of his home and yard. He didn't blow his
leaves off his lawn. Instead, he reversed the motor on his blower and vac-
uumed them up. He should have had his own turf commercial, that's how
green and perfect his lawn was. I've seen many million-dollar properties
with yards not as nice as Jerry's. Everything about his house and property
was perfect. He was also an angel whenever we needed electricity or water,
or to borrow a saw blade. Jerry had helped out the woman who had owned
Case, and I was so happy when he said he would love to have a few pieces of
the furniture left in the house. Danette across the street had a day care, and
her kids would surprise us every day with little gifts. Nothing rid my crew

128

of house renovation grumpiness more than four-year-olds asking them, "What do you get when you cross an elephant and a rhino?" and answering "Elephino!"

As Case stretched on past the six weeks I had expected to spend on it, the fact that I wasn't at Summit every day created tension between Chad and me. He wanted to know when Case was going to be finished, and really, so did I. He was a regular on the Case job site, so he could see that I wasn't intentionally dragging my feet.

By Christmas, we both needed a break. We decided to take a three-day getaway to Puerto Rico, while Ethan spent time with his dad. It would be a quick trip, but sometimes that's all you need to recharge the batteries. The whirlwind vacation did the trick. After three days basking in the Puerto Rican sun and touring every historical site in sight because Chad was a history junkie just like me, I was more in love than ever and ready to get home and get that house done.

The Case rehab picked up speed after I got back. I started ticking one room after another off my list. The period solid-wood pocket doors between rooms on the first floor all slid open and shut like they were brand new. The newly refinished wood floors shimmered in shades of honey and amber. The wainscoting in the kitchen gleamed with new coats of bright white paint, and the new ceiling made the room seem fresh, clean, and inviting.

As we wrapped up the work and filming, I started planning for an open house. Staging one of my houses for the final photo shoots and an open house can be the biggest challenges on the project. If I'm doing it right, it means hunting down the appropriate furniture and accessories. I have to stage rooms so that the house looks lived-in and warm, but not so personal that visitors feel like they are intruding. The decorative elements have to show off the work that's been done, rather than obscure it. Staging is part art and part science—and for me, an obsession that leads to delays in filming and drives Klang and Jose so crazy that if they still had hair, they would pull it out.

Fortunately, we had a lot of great furniture already in the home from the previous owner. But on my show, my houses have always been unlike any other houses out there. It's the details in the staging that wow people. I would never, for example, put a large plant on a coffee table. That's not good enough. Instead I use a period-correct magazine, a planter, and old family photos. With Case, I was able to edit down to pieces that looked appropriate in the space, and I didn't have to buy a lot from outside sources. But while I was working, I had an idea that would gain steam and become the most positive part of that project. I posted an invitation on my social media accounts to any artists who wanted to send art to be shown in the house. I had seen the excitement and pride on my friend Lisa's face when we used her refinished antiques in the Dollar house. And the good news was that the new owner of the Dollar house had loved them so much that he bought most of them from her. I thought, What if we could share that feeling with more people? I had no idea what I had created.

We got artwork from all over the country. Photos, paintings, small sculptures, tapestries, furniture, and things that made me say, "I don't know what it is, just find a place for it." I was buried in submissions, and it became impossible to put a face to any individual piece of art. But it was exciting to open the boxes and see what people had created. I made no guarantee that an artisan would see his or her piece on TV (as I received way more things than I could possibly use to stage the house), and we offered people the option of having the art returned or donating it. That simple plan would lead to one of the most profound moments I've had on *Rehab Addict*.

Fast-forward to 2014. I was working on the Akron house with the professional basketball player LeBron James when I heard a commotion outside. I asked the field producer what was going on, and she said, "Oh, we have some fans here and I'm sending them home. I mean, this is ridiculous. You're working." I stopped her there. That was a big no-no in my world, but she was new to my crew and didn't have a clue. Long before then, my wiser-than-his-years son had said at one of my appearances where an organizer was cutting off our fan line, "If they are taking the time to meet us, Mom, we're going to meet them." (One of his other rules is, quite simply, don't be an asshole. After you get over the shock of that word coming out of your child's mouth, you realize you must've done something right because it's just a modern adaptation of the Golden Rule.) I never lose sight of the fact that people's enthusiasm for my work and my passion has contributed a great deal to my success. I looked out the window and saw a woman in the passenger seat of a car. She was strapped to an oxygen tank. I headed outside and was met by another woman standing by the car.

"Oh my gosh. I'm so sorry, Nicole. My daughter is a huge fan of yours, but it's really difficult for her to get around because she's on oxygen. She's in the car. She just wanted to meet you—we didn't mean to interrupt you." My heart filled. I had been having a trying week there in Akron. We were under an extreme deadline. I had had no sleep, and this surprise visit was just what I never knew I needed.

I opened the car door and started talking with the woman. I didn't know what was ailing her, but she was extremely thin and very weak. Her name was Mina and she had a beautiful smile and eyes that lit up when she talked about watching the show. She noticed the bracelet I was wearing.

"I love that bracelet. It's so pretty."

"Yeah, I love wearing artists' jewelry. My friend Elizabeth made this for me."

"You know what? I sent you photographs I shot for Case."

Mina's art (left). Mina and her mom that day in Akron (right).

"You did?" Now I started feeling bad. With the flood of artwork that had come to Case, it was a mess trying to figure out who'd sent what. Then Mina began describing one of the photos. I touched her arm and stopped her. "Oh, Mina, you don't know how much I love that photo. It's actually in my house now. It's one of my favorite pieces of art."

She beamed at me. We talked and talked, and this young woman brought me back to what matters, and really put life in perspective. She had never gotten the chance to enjoy her teen years or her twenties. She was always in and out of hospitals. But here she was, full of smiles and making art, and she was so positive, so upbeat.

At a point, as Case had dragged on, I had become worn out by the project. But it was wonderful to find that some real good had come out of that house. Mina was an extraordinary woman whom I wouldn't have met if not for Case. We would stay in touch, and I think of her often. Her photo sits in my living room. The necklace I wear with a heart (shaped like the organ, not the symbol) is one of her pieces. It seems like Mina knows when I need a smile, and on those days I'll open my e-mail and there will be a note from her. Or I'll arrive at home after being on the road and find a card—*yes*, an actual card—in the mail, from her or her mom.

When it came time to sell Case, I was ready to pass it on. I only sell my houses to buyers who will value the house and the neighborhood as much as I have. I also add deed restrictions to every house, making sure it can never be torn down, turned into a rental, or chopped up into a multifamily dwelling, and ensuring that the work we did lives on and no neighbor will watch it fall victim to neglect again. Because of the price range, my homes usually attract first-time buyers, and the financing often falls through. I could go on and on about the issues one incurs dealing with buyers, agents, inspectors, and bankers, *oh my*. In the end, it's just one of the things you have to expect in real estate. When a transaction goes smoothly, it's a real surprise, sort of like discovering that an experience with the IRS was actually fun. Case was one of the more challenging transactions for many reasons, and the closing stretched out for months. I was already working in Detroit at that time,

The small bathroom at Case, before (left); with Klang in the tub (center); and after (right).

so Chad stepped in and handled the closing. When I finally met the buyer almost a year later, I was so happy to learn she was a history teacher, of all things. I immediately had the original abstract of title for the house that I had found after closing delivered to her.

Nowadays records of title are boring digital printouts; however, before the existence of computers, titles were beautiful handwritten legal deeds. They would and could list personal details that would never be allowed in a title today. Just as old phone directories listed a person's occupation and even such things as "a single woman," house deed details are quite juicy. I knew the new owner would cherish every second of diving into the history of that home.

Wrapping up Case on such a positive note made me feel in control again. I had delivered a house and a season to the network, and I felt like I'd turned Case into something special. Just the same, the lesson I took away from that house was that I never wanted to give control over my process, my path, to anyone else. It's a lesson I come back to on a regular basis.

*Chapter 5*

# SOMETIMES YOU HAVE TO SKIP THE LEMONADE AND DEAL WITH THE LEMONS

## SUMMIT MANSION

When you have a TV show, people reach out to you all the time. Some send handwritten letters asking for advice on how to fix a water-damaged foundation. Some are fans who shoot me social media posts or e-mails asking to meet me when I'm in their town. Some, though, are downright stalkers. That last group is why I tend not to reply to unsolicited e-mails or text messages that come in out of the blue.

While I was still in the thick of it with Mark, I kept getting e-mails from the assistants of a local businessman. The businessman, Chad, had just bought a large turn-of-the-century house in an old-money part of St. Paul. The neighborhood was stately, an area crowded with impressive stone homes and hundred-year-old trees. Chad's team continued to send me e-mails for months, but I just ignored them. Right or wrong, I had a gut feeling that Mark would see them as something more than a business proposition. When I started on the Dollar house, I got yet another e-mail from Chad's people. This one pitched me on what a great opportunity this house was for me. An opportunity, for me? Seriously? Catch me at the wrong moment and I can be a little flip. I said, "I'll meet this guy for a thousand bucks." Mark had recently changed the locks on Minnehaha, shutting me out of my dream house. I was hustling to get work done on the Dollar house. All in all, I had pretty much lost patience with the world. But Chad's team replied, "No problem," and scheduled a time. I just shook my head. I had no idea they would say okay; that's why I'd thrown out a ridiculous number. Remember, I started my working days making $2.25 an hour, so a thousand bucks to meet me? Silly. And honestly, I didn't have five free minutes, let alone a couple of hours. I canceled. I got a very curt message back. The guy sounded pissed, but oddly, kind of handsome, too, with an accent. Listen, I didn't call the guy back because of the last part; I called him back because I felt bad. And actually, I'm pretty sure I texted him. He said he was stepping into a movie and that he'd get back to me later.

I honestly can't remember how soon after that we spoke. But I remember I was standing in Macy's picking out a tie for Ethan's eighth-grade graduation when Chad called me.

"Listen, I didn't mean to piss you off," I said. "I'm just really, really busy."

He was surprisingly mellow—I could hardly believe it was the same guy who had left the angry voice mail. "No worries."

I said, "So what do you want? I'm not a contractor, and I'm too busy to design any more houses. I don't think I can be much help to you." Without missing a beat, he replied, "I just wanted to take you to dinner." Right there among the rows of tables of ties, in the basement of Macy's in Southdale Center mall, I just stopped, shook my head, and cracked a smile (yes, a genuine one).

"Well, why didn't you just say that to begin with? Because if there's a glass of wine in the cards, I'll be there."

He laughed, and I suggested we meet at the Dollar house for lunch, as the project was still in its early stages and I had no extra time. On the day we were to meet, I had worked all morning, and while everyone else ordered their lunch, I passed because I had plans. Then I got a text from Chad, who was already late, saying he wasn't going to make it. Hungry, hot, and just over it, I thought, Screw this. I grabbed someone's leftover sandwich and went back to work. I had finally called it a day and was at home lying on the couch, melting in my 1904 house with no air-conditioning. I didn't dare go up the three flights of stairs to my fabulous attic master bedroom to take a cool shower. If it was ninety degrees on the main floor, it was surely ten degrees hotter up there. I was wondering how it could possibly be as hot in the house as it was outside when I got a text from Chad saying he was at the Dollar house and asking where I was.

I thought, Seriously, buddy? You make plans, you cancel plans, and then you just show up? It was sounding a bit reminiscent of what I'd just gone through with Mark. I got up off my couch, not even giving a second thought to what I looked like, let alone what I probably smelled like, and rode my Vespa over to Dollar. I think I truly said "What the f@#$?" when I pulled up to the house and there was a Maserati parked in front. I didn't do a good job of hiding my irritation; it seemed a bit ostentatious, considering that the car cost more than many people in the neighborhood could earn in ten years. I showed Chad around the house with a minimum of chatter and a

My Vespa at the job site holding my bag of trash.

cold shoulder. I said a quick good-bye and rode home on my Vespa. He may have asked me about dinner or lunch or to visit Santa Claus for all I know; I was tired, and most of all, I didn't need or want another man whose only self-worth seemed to come in the form of a fancy car and a vanity plate. Yes, a vanity plate.

Was I judging that book by its cover? Without a doubt, yes. I was still reeling from Mark, deep into therapy trying to find the confidence and resolve that I so needed. I knew I had to find myself before I found myself being found by someone else again. Men and women alike often go right back to relationships that mirror the ones they've tried and failed at before, and I was finally ready to stop the cycle. As a girl who was raised in a Catholic family where no one was anyone until they had a someone and all that went with it, I spent most of my life trying to fit into that ideal. A few weeks went by, and just as that Catholic upbringing was always leading me to try to find a husband, it also made me feel guilty. I had behaved rudely when I'd met Chad. I was punishing him for the sins of the other, as he would love to say later on and still says to this day.

I called him and said, "How about we get breakfast?"

I was amazed when I walked in and saw a totally different guy sitting in a window banquette waiting for me. He had been dressed to the nines at the Dollar house, with a designer shirt, a bright banker tie, and a shiny suit. But now he was in casual mode, sporting the kind of graphic-covered, crucifix-themed button-down shirt that you should only wear untucked. The shirt went perfectly with his overpriced, artificially "distressed" bedazzled jeans. Blingy was an understatement. It was not my taste in men's style, but I'll say this for him: He put himself right out there. Chad could not have been more unlike Mark. I found myself laughing as he said, "Wow, you look different." I laughed and asked him what he meant. "Well, you look hot," he said. I said, "Oh, why? Because I showered?" Chad did casual and nonchalant like a talk show host. Given that Mark's two speeds were "intense" and "more intense," it was a refreshing change. Chad talks with his hands, and at one point his large plastic cup of ice water went flying right into his crotch as he was telling a story. He was soaking wet, but I was at ease. Later on, when people would ask how we met, he'd refer to this moment and say, "I spilled water on my crotch and she fell in love."

I said, "Okay, you win. When do you want me to see the house?"

"After I take you to dinner" was the reply and "just friends, no pressure." This was music to my ears and received four cheers from my therapist.

After the heartbreak of Minnehaha, you'd think I'd have learned my lesson; I didn't want to fall in love with another house or another man. I wasn't initially thinking of Chad romantically; as much as some insist that men and women can't just be friends, my experience has proved the opposite. I have a group of single guy friends whom I dine with often. It will break my heart when each one finds "the one," only because I love their company and I have a gut feeling that very few women would understand that our relationship is purely platonic and they'd put an end to it.

He picked me up for dinner at my house the next Saturday. Fancy car, blingy jeans, and, I'm pretty sure, ostrich-skin shoes. I couldn't help but wonder why this man with movie-star good looks had to wear such flashy clothes. Clearly, he didn't know how handsome he was.

I had just received that promised glass of wine when he said, "What happened with this last guy?" I gave him the short of it, and he looked at me and said, "I want to get married and I'd love more children. Now that that's out of the way, what else should we discuss?" As the dinner went on, I felt more and more relaxed. We talked about motorcycles, antique cars—he seemed to hit on every one of my interests.

After dinner, we drove over to the house. It was hot—no AC—and it smelled like dog pee. Still, the 1904 mansion felt like a sumptuous trip back in time, with mahogany everywhere, detailed built-ins filling every room, coffered ceilings, and incredible leaded-glass windows throughout. It had seven bedrooms and five fireplaces. The seven-car garage was hidden by old-growth landscaping from the huge pool that looked like it had just been dropped from the sky into the middle of a forest. The massive trees created an impression of utter privacy. As I made my way through the house, I was mesmerized.

"Oh my gosh. It's so beautiful. It's just so beautiful," I kept muttering.

When we reached the top floor of the house, Chad said, "I'm sorry. I didn't hear what you were saying; I was staring at your bum." I laughed and smiled.

After the grand tour, he asked me to tackle the house and I told him, in no uncertain terms, *no*. All that beauty hid some major problems. Summit's age had taken its toll. The mechanicals were pretty much shot. It was going to need major electrical work, a ton of new plumbing, and a whole lot more. The hardwood floors were overdue for refinishing, and the house had a tired look that called for some serious cosmetic magic. The kitchen, dining room, and bedrooms also needed to be updated and brought back to life.

The big issue, though, was the water damage in the basement. That damage needed fixing right away. Chad looked dismayed. "But the inspector said it was nothing."

"The inspector was wrong," I told him.

He told me he had found a contractor whom he trusted to do the work, but he needed someone who had an overall vision for the house. He asked me if I would at least come on as a consultant. I told him no again. I had given him my input on the house, and I had already done the boyfriend-as-partner-in-a-house thing. Once was enough, but always a glutton for punishment, I had more than my share of those experiences. No thank you.

I knew Chad needed to find someone who cared about the house; I just didn't want it to be me. Unfortunately, what he had instead was an assistant who thought she was a designer. She decided that if she didn't take action, nothing was going to happen with this "old fossil" of a house. Unbeknownst to Chad, she had a contractor come in the following Monday morning, dragging along his jackhammer, pry bars, and anything else that could wreak destruction. In the space of a day, he destroyed two bathrooms—a first-floor powder room and a second-floor full bath. Gone was the amazing subway tile. Gone were the period fixtures. Gone was everything. It was disgusting. As I would later say on the *Rehab Addict* episode featuring the restoration of the destroyed powder room: "If you have to use a jackhammer to get bathroom tile out, the tile isn't meant to come out."

I was shocked at the devastation one contractor could do in a day. After we looked at the damage, staring at stripped rooms that looked like ragged wounds on the body of the house, Chad and I walked out back to get some air and talk about next steps. I was horrified and so was he. I said I would set him up with my tradespeople, but that was it. I was working like crazy on the Dollar house and I couldn't handle any extra house drama. My

One of the destroyed bathrooms at Summit.

tradespeople met with him, and little by little, I got sucked into the house. At the Dollar house, Chad became the favorite among the Ladies That Paint, as he would regularly show up in a suit with trays full of Starbucks teas and cookies. Then, to our surprise, he would start working alongside us. Was he the handiest of guys? No, but not many of them are. But I think when you are a man and you walk onto a job site where there's a woman you are after and she's driving a Bobcat, you have two choices: be confident enough to say, "I'm absolutely cool with this and not intimidated by her working with a crew of men or that she could build the Taj Mahal if she wanted to," or become insecure and act out. Chad chose the former.

The Dollar house was ahead of schedule. And against every single person on Earth's advice, I told Chad I would help him with the Summit mansion. Just the kitchen, though. He was elated. Justin said, "Girl, I hope you know what you're doing." I assured him I did. Looking back, yes, I should have said no, but I was feeling so confident with the Dollar house that I thought I could do anything. Plus, the Summit house was amazing, and the truth was, this guy was winning me over.

While the Dollar house was speeding along, Ethan was back from Michigan preparing for a new school year. My birthday was right around the corner. On the actual day, I was just getting ready to go to the lake with Ethan when I got a call. It was Chad. He said, "Listen, I got you something for your birthday, but there's a problem. So you need to meet me at the side of the road of

My 1962 Chevy truck.

Highway 5 toward Minnetonka." He gave me the intersection, and not knowing what to expect, Ethan and I loaded up in the car and headed out. At said intersection was Chad with a 1962 Chevy truck. As I drove up, I thought, Did this guy buy me a truck? No, that's just crazy. Imagine my surprise when Chad said, "Happy birthday, I bought you a truck." And then he handed me the title and said, "Before you say anything, it's in your name, no games." I was speechless. The bad news was, something had blown in the truck while he was driving it to me. But the good news was, I got to sit in it before they loaded it up onto the flatbed. The truck was gone for months. While it was in the shop, I had seatbelts added after a concerned Ethan said, "What, there are no seatbelts? Are you going to tell me there are no airbags either?"

I have never received another gift like it; it's still parked in my garage. I drive the truck once a year out of nostalgia. As time has passed, on the worst days with Chad, one look at that truck and I remember the guy I fell in love with and that moment when he made me feel like the only woman in the world for him.

Around this time, I got a call from Beth, a close friend of mine.

She said, "Hey, Nicole. I have a friend whose husband is battling brain cancer. He's a huge fan. It would mean the world to him if he could tour one of your houses with you."

I thought, Well, if he likes old houses, he's going to love Summit. I asked Chad if he could come over, and he said, "No problem!"

On a Saturday afternoon, a car pulled up on the side of Summit and out stepped Kristi and her husband, Art. Art's head was shaved and covered with a patchwork of scars from surgery to operate on a brain tumor. The surgery, the tumor, or both had left him unable to speak. But he could move around, so I brought him into the house. From the minute he walked in, his eyes lit up.

A lot of people can't deal with someone who is terminally ill. We don't do a good job of that in our society. Most people don't know how to react around someone like Art. They become visibly uncomfortable and won't look at the person, or they end up talking *at* them as if they're hard of hearing instead of sick and infirm.

I led Art around the house and just talked to him, anticipating the questions anyone would ask if they were interested in what I was doing. I knew he understood what I was saying, and I could see the delight in his eyes as he walked into each new room. It was obvious to me that Art was an "old house" person, too. He got what I was doing and why.

The next day, Beth sent me a text thanking me. "You have no idea how much that meant to him. That was so awesome." I thought, Heck, it was an hour out of my day, and the best hour I spent all week.

Me at Summit.

Two weeks later, Beth e-mailed me. Art, Kristi, and their two teen-agers lived in an old house that was also serving as Art's hospice. They were crowded for room. The kids didn't have any space to call their own, so Art and Kristi wanted to find someone to redo their basement on the cheap. She was hoping that I could recommend an inexpensive contractor. Money was tight, as it is for most people who are fighting cancer or any major medi-cal disaster. The myth is that insurance covers everything. The truth is, it doesn't, and that's the least of it. Medical bills are one thing, but mortgage companies and electric companies don't care if you have cancer and mount-ing medical bills; they still want to get paid. I knew that any contractor was going to wind up charging them a going rate, and it would probably be more than they could afford. So I arranged to stop by and check out the basement. I took measurements and then e-mailed all my contractors. I told them the story of Art.

Everyone agreed to chip in. I met with Kristi and told her, "Look, you're not going to get a hundred-thousand-dollar remodel. But we're going to give you a brand-new family room, redo the bathroom downstairs, make it a usable space, and do our spin on the house." She was super grateful, and every day I spent in that house reminded me how important family and love are. What I had also found out was that during his cancer battle, Art had become a huge fan of HGTV and DIY Network. I thought, How cool would it be for Art to see his house on TV? I approached Kristi with the idea and made it very clear that they didn't have to say yes and that I wasn't there to exploit them. I just thought it might be cool to have them on the show. She laughed and said absolutely.

Art became such a vibrant part of our lives that it was impossible to keep in mind that he was dying. I would come through the door in the morning and he would be sitting there watching a *Rehab Addict* marathon. He knew I hated hearing my own voice and he loved to tease me and wind me up. I'd say, "Art, what are you watching? You're killing me here, man." He'd laugh and turn it off. Art was a dream. He and Kristi had the kind of marriage that every couple wants. I'm sure it wasn't perfect—whose is?—but as much as Art was the kind of man that every woman wants for her kids, and every child wants for a dad, Kristi was his rock. She was so caring and obviously madly in love with Art and their children. Everyone who knew them loved them. Art was a talented musician and a woodworker, and it seemed like there was nothing he couldn't do.

Except throw stuff out. The basement was crammed full of old house parts that Art had collected over the better part of twenty years. I even found a chalkboard with "Art—clean up poop" written on it. Kristi laughed when she saw it. She had written that reminder when she was pregnant with their son. He was now thirteen.

There were so many laughs on that project. I hope our being there every day just kind of created a positive chaos for Art. When someone is

Art's basement, before (left) and almost done (right).

sick, a house can become like a big vacuum of darkness with curtains drawn and everything quiet. But dying people don't need to be reminded that they're dying; I feel they need to be reminded that they're still very much alive. With that being said, Art's house was still my work site, and I rarely use my inside voice. Too often I would come running up the stairs talking, accidentally waking Art, and I always felt bad.

We had only a couple of days left before the basement was going to be completed. I was just leaving for the day to go pick up Ethan at school when Kristi stopped me and said, "Do you want to go up and talk to Art?"

I asked, "Is he sleeping?"

"He's in and out."

"Then I don't want to wake him up. I'll talk to him tomorrow."

"Oh, okay."

What I didn't understand was that I think Kristi knew the end was near, and maybe it was her way of asking me if I wanted to say good-bye to

Art. Maybe it wasn't, but now having witnessed "the end" more times than anyone ever should, I know firsthand that loved ones seem to have an innate sense of when that time is near. After seeing him every day for almost eight weeks, I just couldn't wrap my head around the fact that he was going to die. But at five the next morning, I got the news that Art had passed away.

I called everyone on my crew, and it was kind of like time stopped. We had all had so much fun on that project, and Art had been the center of that fun. None of us really thought that day would come. It's crazy, but that's the way it is. You think all lemons will eventually become lemonade, but sometimes they're just lemons.

A few weeks earlier, my friend Lauren had arranged for a photographer who specializes in sensitive situations to take pictures of the family. The photographer came in, and within twenty minutes (Art was so very weak), she captured the essence of this beautiful family.

I wanted to design the basement as the story of Art's world, of what mattered in his life. We ended up using a lot of what he had kept in the basement as decoration. I designed around the chalkboard. I hung Art's old bicycles on the walls. We got the family a pool table and used it as a centerpiece for what would be a very cool, relaxing room for years to come. We sent the photographer's images off to a company to print them on wall-sized canvases.

Ironically, a few days after Art had passed, the canvases showed up. They were huge. So there we were, all of us in the basement. As I pulled the brown paper off the first of the photos, suddenly there was Art, with his wonderfully expressive eyes, staring back at us. This scene is one of the only times I have broken the fourth wall (as it's called in the television world when you show the show). The camera panned and caught images of me and my crew. We were trying to be brave, but we were missing our friend. We hung the photos and left that house full of love and memories.

After Art passed, Beth had a T-shirt made up for me with one of my favorite catchphrases, "Old houses, old people, old dogs." It was a tribute to the connection I had with Art. Selling those T-shirts in memory of him has allowed us to raise thousands of dollars for families like his. I was left with fond memories of Art and boxes and boxes of his old house parts. By this time, the plan to just stop at the kitchen renovation at Summit had fallen by the wayside. I had taken on the Case house and while we were busy over there, the major structural issues at Summit were being addressed. And honestly, this break from Summit gave me a chance to catch my breath.

Gramps in his favorite T-shirt.

I wanted Summit to be fantastic, to achieve all the potential it had in its pedigree. It was so majestic that I fought the feeling that I had bitten off more than I could chew at that moment. It was an odd feeling, and not at all like me. I have total faith in my abilities, and I had just rocked the Dollar house in record time. But it seemed like a far different animal from Summit. It's one thing to restore a small house in a rough neighborhood. It's something entirely different when you're starting with a house that has a market value upward of two million dollars.

It didn't help that the area was crowded with moneyed, pompous, privileged people. Everyone in St. Paul seemed to know that I was doing the house and there was a lot of buzz that I was going to fall on my face.

People love to see a high-profile person fail. I had set the bar high and was obsessed with keeping Summit historically correct.

I was still trying to wrap my head around fixing bathrooms that the contractor had gutted. My struggle was that I had seen the original bathrooms and loved them. Nothing in my mind could compete, so my vision was blocked. One day, while digging through Art's stock of old house parts, I came across two old cat litter buckets full of porcelain octagonal tile. I have no idea where he got it, but when I saw it, I realized those tiles might be a perfect match for the powder room at Summit . . . and they were. I don't think I ever shared with Chad where the "new" tile had come from—all I was focused on was that Art would probably get a good laugh knowing that his "junk" had made it into the mansion.

That solved one bathroom, but we

E waiting for me at Summit (top). Filming (bottom).

still had the massive hole of destruction where the grand master bathroom had once been. Every time Chad and I would walk the house, huffing and puffing from floor to floor, he would joke about installing an elevator. We quickly sized everything up and to our surprise, there was an empty pocket in the middle of the house. Had the master bath been intact, we would have never dreamed of rearranging it to make room for an elevator, but now it was gone, and I thought, Well, that's one way to fix this. Installing an elevator is no small feat. I was amazed at how it was built. It seemed to take forever.

The truth was, every day I spent in that house, Chad and I would add on something more extravagant and more fabulous to the home, which meant it just kept getting further and further behind schedule. I had promised the Summit mansion to the network for season four and was missing deadline after deadline. It wasn't good. In very simple terms, if I wanted to keep my job (by this time, the show had become my main source of income), I had to find a solution to delivering episodes fast, and a never-ending Summit mansion renovation wasn't going to do it.

I made some calls, and Brian, whom I'd met at the Dollar house, had some ideas. Three properties in north Minneapolis could be had fairly easily. Just like that, I was off and running. Chad was on the verge of a heart attack.

Installing Art's tile in the powder room.

The Summit pool, before (top, left). Getting pulled into the pool by Ethan
(top, right). The renovated pool (bottom).

Within a few weeks, I closed on the 4th Street and 25th Avenue houses (I had my sights on Hillside Avenue as well, but that would take another two years to come to fruition, and the details would require another book). I thought I had finally created the perfect model for how to shoot *Rehab Addict* as the two houses were within a few blocks of each other so we filmed them simultaneously. It was nuts. Chad grew more resentful with every swing of a hammer I took at the other properties. I was still overseeing everything going on at Summit, but it didn't seem to matter. At one point, I said, "Why aren't you over there managing Summit full-time? It's your house!" I was doing what I should be doing—focusing on my own business and career— but I was made to feel guilty. The truth was, Chad had a very easy "do whatever the heck I want routine," and I didn't. I had done what everyone had warned me against and once again mixed business with pleasure. And now I was paying the price. I wanted to leave my job site and get swept off my feet, but the romantic, "Let me spoil you" Chad was long gone. With one angry phone call, he called it quits.

My heart was broken, and upon finishing the 4th Street house, I found solace in setting my sights on a new challenge: Detroit (more on that later). And as fate would have it, I eventually came back to Summit. This time not as the girlfriend, but as the designer. There were attorneys involved, and we signed a contract so that we could use the house on television. And again, did I know better? Yes,

Working on the pool bathroom with Nick and Dave.

but I knew disaster would come to that house at the hands of anyone else, and deep down, I missed Chad. He was and still is a pain, but in the moments he isn't, he's great.

When I first came back to Summit, we didn't speak. Not a word. I just worked on the house, which was turning out to be absolutely beautiful. With each room nearing completion, my heart melted. I remembered the first time I was there. I remembered my funny "mister," as I called him, saying, "Forget about Minnehaha; this is yours." We started dating again. My crew was exasperated, saying, "Love him, hate him, we don't care; let's just finish the house." And of course, within the amount of time it took for the floors to dry, Chad and I ended up being back at each other's throats. I felt unappreciated; he felt neglected.

Dave and me pretending to shoot. He's saying to me, "Just a few more days; you've got this."

The house, with the exception of the kitchen, the master suite, and the basement, was almost complete. I had the furniture in. It felt like everything was coming together as we were falling apart. We were fighting, I was working, and Chad? Well, the kindest way to put it is that he was seeking a way to not feel neglected.

Here I was putting every bit of energy I had into this house—his house—and in return he was spending his days telling everyone how horrible I was. His favorite word to describe me was "dismissive." I would retort dismissively, "How

Filming the walk-through for Summit, Dave and Andrew wore construction vests to try to get me to laugh.

have you not figured out that my attitude is a direct result of your decision to treat me like your contractor instead of your girlfriend?" A common misconception about strong women is that we don't need the hand-holding, the flowers, and the nice gestures, and what I've found to be true is that it's the strong women who want it the most. I took a long hard look at the relationship and realized it still wasn't right after all these years.

I finished the rooms I had been working on, and I packed my things to go back to Detroit. During the summer, it became apparent (due to contractual obligations) that I would indeed have to return to Summit because after more than a year, that damn elevator had finally shown up and I needed to film it being installed to close out the episodes. Chad thought for sure that meant I would be staying on to finish the house. Had he responded the way I'd hoped to some news I would soon receive, I most definitely would have, but in the end, that was the last time I would work on the Summit mansion. He was convinced that I would edit the show to make it appear that I had finished the renovation, but I didn't. I told the truth.

It wasn't done, but I was reluctantly moving on. Chad had no choice but to take over the "design" of the house. I was called incompetent by every Tom, Dick, and Harry he had working in there after me, of course. Unfortunately, homeowners who have a beef with their previous contractors are magnets for contractors who see an easy dollar to be made. They remind me of divorce attorneys; the rich ones only get that way by keeping their clients fighting.

The fact was, I could have just taken it on the chin and tried to make lemonade out of Summit. But instead, I worked with the lemons. Someone else's lemons. I never had an open house for Summit, and I don't like to talk about it. The sour aftertaste of lemons is what keeps me focused these days, anytime I might be tempted to consider taking on a house that someone else owns.

*Chapter 6*

# PASSION ALLOWS THE PHOENIX TO RISE FROM THE ASHES

## CAMPBELL STREET PROJECT

I went back to Detroit not just to distract myself from my broken heart, but also to snap myself out of the monotony that I felt *Rehab Addict* and my life had become. While the 4th Street project and the 25th Avenue houses were great, they didn't quite ignite a fire in me. 4th Street hit the market and sold right away. 25th Avenue? It was just about finished when I saw something I couldn't resist: a Curbed.com advertisement for firehouses for sale in Detroit. Imagine living in an old firehouse! I was sure one of them would make an incredible project for the show, and a terrific single-family dwelling that could be the centerpiece of a neighborhood springing back to life.

RT @freep #Detroit to sell 7 vacant firehouses, renovated police facility on.freep.com/18tfktf
Cc: @NCRehabAddict

5/8/13, 7:13 AM

**Detroit to sell 7 vacant firehouses, renovated police facility**

Detroit is selling seven unused firehouses and a renovated but long-vacant police facility that once housed horses in a move to raise money and encourage redevelopment in a city bleeding cash and...

Detroit Free Press @freep

The tweet that started the firehouse search.

So I sat down and wrote a long e-mail to the network and pitched Detroit—specifically, a firehouse.

It wasn't going to be an easy sell. Former Detroit mayor Kwame Kilpatrick had just been convicted of corruption and was in prison. The city had no money. Neighborhoods were devastated in the wake of the real estate bubble bursting. Homeowners were being evicted for back taxes. Bailiffs would show up in the morning, and by the afternoon, former owners would be standing on the sidewalk with dazed looks on their faces and their possessions in dumpsters. There were blocks upon blocks of empty houses, with broken windows and overgrown yards. It was the very definition of blight. Banks were foreclosing with no plan in place and then letting the houses sit empty and fall apart. I had my work cut out for me. The whole world looked at Detroit like a wasteland.

I'm always a bit surprised when I see projects listed on the Internet and the phone number actually goes to a live person. I get sent hundreds of "Nicole, check out this house" e-mails a week, and honestly, very few are legit. The person on the other end of the phone in Detroit introduced himself as James. When I inquired about the firehouses, he launched into a diatribe, describing each one. I stopped him and said I would check them out for myself.

It's such an easy commute from Minneapolis to Detroit, I could be there within two hours. On the day I'd arranged to meet with James, my mom picked me up at the curb outside Detroit Metropolitan arrivals. She was as excited as I was. In those days, the show and the houses were still very much a family affair, and my mom knew that if we grabbed a firehouse, it would bring me one step closer to calling Detroit home again.

As we drove east on I-94, I felt so excited. The city of Detroit might have looked abandoned to anyone else, but I envisioned it as the bustling metropolis it had once been, with the beautiful stores downtown that my grandparents always told me stories about. We pulled up to Cadillac Tower, where James's office was located, and parked right out front. (One advantage of a broken city is the ample parking.)

Cadillac Tower has a little shop in the entry and beautiful brass doors and elevators, but the rest of the building had gotten a "makeover" in the 1980s, and what big hair and neon did for fashion, mauve carpeting and drop ceilings did for design. I called James from the lobby and he answered. At any minute, I expected this adventure to go bust. I mean, it couldn't seriously be this easy, could it? A few minutes later, a tall man in a tan suit, very business-like, approached us with keys in his hand and said, "Nicole? Let's go."

I said, "James?"

And he said, "Yeah." And then there was an awkward pause.

"We can just follow you," I told him.

"I have a city van. This way we can talk and you won't get lost," he explained.

I didn't argue; I got the feeling you just went with what James said. And I love seeing how situations like this play out. In a life where I have to take charge of just about everything, it's refreshing when someone else has a plan. And James had a plan, all right. What I soon found out about James—the voice on the end of that 313 extension—was that he wasn't just a fly-by-night city employee. James—James Marusich—headed up Detroit's Planning and

Development Department. He had seen it all. He had been around since the Mayor Coleman Young administration, a time when I was dealing with multiplication tables and wearing jelly shoes. Through all the bureaucracy over the years, James had managed to do something unheard of: He had stayed on the city payroll through several administration changes.

The city van was, without a doubt, the best representation of what was wrong in our beloved Detroit. It was caked with layers of dirt and road grime, which covered the paint and hid a patchwork of dents. The brakes were barely there and the heater was on the fritz. The city seal on the outside had seen better days. I get carsick at the drop of a hat, which is why I insist on being in the driver's seat whenever I travel. But I was going to have to grin and bear it as we headed off to the far corners of the city in search of the next *Rehab Addict* project.

I had started the trip with my usual optimism, assuming we'd find structures exactly as the firefighters had left them. I had imagined that these structures would be clean and bare, and would only need to be converted into a residence, not necessarily rebuilt from scratch. Silly me.

We drove in a zigzag pattern all over the city. I didn't have a good sense of where we were at any given point because it was pouring rain. But my fantasy of a firehouse located right downtown started fading soon; each one was located farther out and in a more desolate part of the city. The locations were bad enough, but the biggest shock was the state of the firehouses.

By the time we walked through the fourth firehouse, my romantic notions were gone. I was wet, hungry, nauseated, and cold. Even my mom was losing steam. If you lose both of us, it's never a good thing. The firehouse in the Mt. Elliott section of the city was one I'd had high hopes for as I knew this area and my grandmother had spent the majority of her childhood in an orphanage around the corner. It's not far from the Detroit River and the

My romantic idea of firehouses was shattered.

setting, I'm sure, was absolutely picturesque eighty years ago. We opened the doors and it was a mess, just like all the others. Trash was piled up in the fire truck bays. The place had been vandalized. The windows were broken out. The walls were bashed in or spray-painted with nasty comments about the new fire commissioner and other choice sayings you wouldn't want your children to read. The large garage doors were jammed half open, and everything else in the place was in disrepair.

I always look past the bad and focus on one good thing. A project just needs one thing to get me inspired: a fireplace mantel, an original sink, even a bit of hardwood flooring. During this whole process, I had focused on the fire pole. I was heartbroken when I learned there were none. No fire poles? They had been deemed obsolete and removed years ago. I told James that had he told me that when I called, I would have stayed home. He said matter-of-factly, "You didn't ask." No fire pole, complete devastation, risky chance for resell, and the city still wanted twenty to sixty thousand dollars for a firehouse.

James sensed my defeated spirit and asked if I minded if he took me on a detour. He drove though Brush Park.

"Nicole, forget the firehouses," he said with a twinkle in his eye. I said earlier that this man had a plan, and he did. He parked in front of the Ransom Gillis mansion, a dilapidated but still beautiful 1800s house with a turret—in other words, my dream home. He took me through the interior and I was in love. Looking back, I realize that James was a great salesman. He saved the best for last, knowing I would leap through the house like a child toward a puppy they didn't know they were getting.

I started doing the budget in my head, and we discussed the house all the way back to his office. When James finally dropped us at my mom's car, I told him, "I'll give it some thought and get back to you." But I already knew that as much as I loved the Ransom Gillis mansion, at that time, it was a no-go. I love saving old houses, but I'm still a mom who has a family to think about. Paying even a penny for any of these buildings at the time was too much. That wasn't the last of James or the Ransom Gillis mansion, but I didn't know that then.

My mom and I decided to have lunch before I flew out. I did the numbers over and over again. My budget wouldn't work. I was in a panic, to say the least. I had sold Detroit to the network. I couldn't go home empty-handed. Sometimes, desperation leads to brilliance. And if there was any time I needed it, it was then. I started brainstorming. And just like that, a name popped into my head: Rosie Mackenzie.

Rosie Mackenzie was a fan from Detroit who had written letters, e-mails—I'm pretty sure the birds outside my window were carrying messages from her: "Nicole, you have to see this house." I finally called her one day just to say, "No, I'm sorry." But she managed to win me over with niceness and promised, "I'm not a crazy stalker."

Now I was desperate, and it just might be Rosie's lucky day. I frantically searched through my phone and realized I didn't have her number. I was out of time. I sat there in disbelief. Then I recalled having asked Justin to check out the house if he was ever in the neighborhood. Justin had worked on the Dollar house with me but was now living back in Detroit.

I called Justin and asked, "Any chance you have the number of that woman with the house in Detroit?"

Justin has a habit of making a noise that I can't quite describe, but it's a mix between clearing his throat, laughing, and screaming.

"Rosie's? Nicole, what are you up to? That house is a mess. It has a burned-down house lying on top of it. There's nothing there."

"Just give me the number!" I told him. I felt like Nancy Drew finally getting that last clue. I repeated the number out loud and my mom wrote it down on a napkin. I quickly dialed it, and Rosie answered. Later on I would realize what a miracle this was, because Rosie never ever answers her phone. Finally, something was going right.

She couldn't have sounded more excited when she picked up the phone and found out I was calling her about the house. "I have to be honest, Rosie.

The Campbell Street project, before (left) and after (right).

I'll swing by, but I'm not making any promises." I certainly didn't want to break this woman's heart; she had waited almost a year for me to come by, but I knew I had no time and if it wasn't great, I'd have to walk away. Thankfully, the address she gave me—Campbell Street North—was on the way to the airport. "Make sure you put in the North or you won't find it," she warned. I didn't know the area, but I could still make my flight and see the house; this seemed perfect to me.

I pulled up in front of a 1929 Tudor that was in bad, bad shape. The yard was overgrown, and the house looked like it was about to tumble over. Rosie came bustling up to me as I got out of the car. She was adorable, like everybody's favorite aunt. She had a big-as-life smile and sparkling eyes. She looked like a young Kathy Bates. She started crying and hugged me.

"I'm so glad you came. My mom just loved your show. Me too."

I asked, "Where's your mom?"

With that question, more tears came and I got a sinking feeling.

When she was able to compose herself, she explained, "She passed away three weeks ago. It was her dream to have you rehab the house. It would have meant everything to her that you came." And that was it. I felt horrible. Here this woman had been writing to me for a year on behalf of her mother, Dorothy, and I had missed meeting her by three weeks. At that moment, I knew that whether I took on the project or not, I would do whatever I could to ease the burden of the house for Rosie.

We walked up the cracked walkway to the front door with Rosie talking a mile a minute about how much her mother would have loved to see me there, and how much she wanted me to do the house. Her elderly father, Art, still lived across the street, so she was there daily. Old people and an old house. She was killing me with this stuff. The scene would only have been more complete if she'd had an old rescue dog with cataracts.

When I stepped into the living room, my stomach churned. Standing there, I could see that the damage was extensive. The smell was actually a bit refreshing after the stench of the firehouses. Not rotting and horrible, but smoky like a campfire. The house next door had caught fire and fallen onto this one, spreading the flames. Downstairs, just past the dining room, the whole back of the house was missing. Upstairs, most of the roof had been burned

The Campbell Street house exterior with the burned-out neighboring house, before (top) and after (bottom).

The only room that wasn't burned was the living room, before (top) and after (bottom).

away, and what was left needed to be entirely replaced. Almost half the house was gone. Everything that was left intact had twenty layers of soot on it. The plaster walls were streaked where the water from the fire hoses had made its way down.

At moments like these, I always look for the diamonds in the dirt. The house had flashes of beautiful detailing. There were incredible plaster medallions on the ceilings and wonderfully detailed archways between rooms. The hardwood floors were charred, but they could be revived. The house would need new windows and doors, as it had none, but the bones were still okay. Ten minutes in that house after a long day of disappointment, and I had a good feeling. The truth was, that house—my soon-to-be Campbell house—had a lot of love surrounding it. I felt it and, more important, I needed it.

"Rosie, I've got to get to the airport. But I want you to know, I'm going to figure this out." I thought she was going to break my bones with the hug she gave me.

But as soon as I settled into my seat on the plane, my mind started racing. I had just agreed to take on a burned-out wreck of a house from a woman who rightfully anticipated I'd return it to its former glory. Had I done it because I needed to be a hero? I took a deep breath and thought it through. No, I didn't need to be a hero. I knew that this house was as much a risk as anything else I had seen that day, but the difference was that this one would be a twofer: not only would I save a house, but I'd help Rosie and her family heal from losing their mom.

By the time I arrived at the dreaded G22 gate at Minneapolis–St. Paul International Airport, I was thinking I was either an adventurous genius or a naive idiot. It didn't matter either way; I felt relieved that I had something concrete to back up my pitch to the network, and this wasn't the first time I jumped into something I had no clue about.

A few years earlier, I kept seeing banners for the Tri-Loppet triathlon. Every day, I would run from my door around the chain of lakes and back. Well, I just told a big fib. *Once in a while*, I would run the chain of lakes, but most of the time it was simply down around Lake Calhoun and back, which is just under five miles. Most people think Minneapolis and think below-zero temps, but as soon as summer hits, it's hot. I checked out the race online

Sarah paints a medallion (left). This is what we call a "Detroit skylight" (right).

and was intrigued. It wasn't a traditional tri where you swim, bike, and run. In this one, you paddle, bike, and run. Why's that a big deal? I don't swim so well. I get in the water, and while I appear skilled for thirty seconds, I have never really finessed the art of swimming, and I have a fear of sticking my face under water. So this kind of tri was made for me. I signed up and found a partner to canoe with for the paddle portion.

The morning of the race, I was up early and I was nervous wondering if I'd be able to complete the race. It was my first triathlon. I had a little coffee for some extra pep and was on my way. When I arrived, I asked for my canoe, and I was told with a shrug by one of the organizers, "We're out of canoes." I looked at him and waited. No more words came out of his mouth. Usually when you tell someone something like that, there's a second part . . . the solution. Instead, he said, "Don't know what to tell you. We do have kayaks." A kayak? I had never kayaked, and the kicker was, there wasn't a double kayak; it was simply a single. So if I wanted to race that day, I was on my own.

I carefully slid my rental kayak into the cold, glassy water and watched as it bobbed from side to side, making little ripples. It certainly didn't look

very stable, but I slipped in as gracefully as possible—which is to say, none too gracefully—settled myself, and started paddling. It was a real embrace-your-fear moment. All the things that could go wrong raced through my mind. But I was already sitting in this shaky little boat, and now I was committed. I made my way along slowly, trying to ignore the nasty looks I got from the more experienced paddlers who were passing

Competing in my first triathlon.

me left and right. Yes, it may have taken me an hour to cover the picturesque route across Lake Calhoun to Lake of the Isles and on to the shore of Cedar Lake, but I did it. And I wasn't even the last one to finish! I went on to bike and run the rest of the triathlon, but it was the kayaking that really stuck with me. The part that might have kept me away in the first place is now a favorite pastime of mine. I have my own kayak, and I love going out on the lake at the end of a hectic day. So tackling a burned-out house? No problem.

That doesn't mean I wasn't scared. To be honest, I was terrified. I knew that whatever money I threw into this house, I probably wasn't going to get back. This was simply a means-to-an-end kind of house. I wanted to go back to Detroit, and this house would be perfect for the show. And in no way, shape, or form was I looking at it as an investment.

At the time, no one wanted to film in Detroit (unless you were a news station looking for a down-and-out story). But I had discovered that with the network, as with so much in business, it's always best to present solutions rather than problems. I didn't tell the network that I'd found a burned-out house in a challenging inner-city area. I didn't ask them what they thought about bringing a crew to a neighborhood in Detroit. No, instead I sent them an impassioned mission statement in the form of an episode guide entirely thought out from start to finish. I described exactly how these powerful episodes would unfold, what we would shoot for each one, and how the stages would come together. It would be just the greatest thing ever. They didn't have to do anything but say yes and promote the episodes when I was done.

Sending the e-mail was easy. The network actually gave the project the green light. Getting everything else planned, however, was a little more difficult.

Jose would be joining me in Michigan, and Justin was already there. People in Detroit expected trailers to roll in with lights and a production

My return to Detroit.

crew. They were sorely disappointed to find out it was just the three of us. As for contractors? We would be starting from scratch.

Ethan was on board as we spent the summers back and forth between Detroit and Minneapolis anyhow. He wished me good luck but assured me he would not be in Detroit on-site without water, electricity, or even a bathroom in the scorching heat saving a house. No, he would be an hour north hanging with my parents, most likely in the pool with my mom, hiking with my dad, or locked in on Xbox. The little boy who begged to have his own tools was now a teenager. My work was no longer intriguing to him.

The priority was to track down the owner of the burned-out house next door to the Campbell Street house, as it was literally lying on top of it and we couldn't do any work until that house was gone. I had hoped the owner could get somebody to demolish it and cart away the wreckage. But the house was in a kind of bureaucratic limbo. Technically, there *was* no owner. That mysterious "somebody" I had hoped to find would have to be me.

The project called for roofers, plasterers, a carpenter, an electrician, a plumber, painters, and more. Unfortunately, it turned out that the biggest challenge of the Campbell Street house wasn't going to be the work itself.

I could figure out how to rebuild a burned structure and repair just about anything. The hardest part was going to be getting the professionals I needed to come to Detroit.

Even for top dollar, no one wanted any part of driving to Campbell Street. I called everyone I knew, and everyone they knew in Detroit. I was already racing the clock and I hadn't even found a roofer. I called dozens of companies and couldn't even get someone to come out and give an estimate.

One day I was having lunch at Woodbridge Pub and the owner came over to tell me he loved my work. I told him about my project, and he asked me how it was going.

"If I can ever find a roofer who will work here, I'll let you know," I told him.

"Sammy does roofs," he said as he disappeared into the kitchen. He came back with Sammy. He was the cook who had just made my lunch. He did roofing on the side, and he had no problem working in the city. He lived in the city. So just like that, I had a roofer. That was all I needed to get my momentum back. Justin and I tracked down another friend we grew up with to do the electrical, and Justin found a plumber and landscapers, which wasn't even on our list. I didn't have a budget for landscaping and said, "Why did you find a landscaper? Really, Justin?"

And with that laugh-scream-clear-the-throat thing, he said, "Relax. The landscaper knew I was working with you and offered to pitch in." Lynn and Glenn at Four Seasons Garden Center were my first "we love what you are doing and want to be a part of it" company in Detroit. I was on cloud nine.

For the most part, the project was looking up, but not as far as the weather was concerned. It rained so much, I actually thought about giving up on the house and building an ark instead. Even when it looked like a

The heat had melted the paint off the walls, but the glorious fixtures and the tile survived—
as did the original medicine cabinet and mirror!

clear day, we'd just get started on the roof when all of a sudden dark clouds
and lightning would move in and there would be yet another downpour.
We wouldn't have enough time to get the tarps back in place. Every time
it rained, I watched something else in the house get damaged by the water.
It was late June before it finally let up and we could really get moving on
the renovation.

In the meantime, I hired a guy named Ratty to demolish and remove
what was left of the house next door. He was in his sixties and was another
friend of a friend who told me that when he got done fishing, he would pay
a visit. Ratty kept his word and rolled onto Campbell Street with his truck,
trailer, and excavator. He got out with his lunch box in one hand and flip
phone in the other, and said, pointing at the excavator, "I'm climbing in
and won't climb out for six hours." He cleared that lot with a determination that I recognized, and I knew Ratty was one of those salt-of-the-earth
guys that remind me of Gramps—no bullshit. And when he was done, the

house was gone and the lot was cleared, but due to the rain, I was left with a big mud pit.

During it all, Rosie's visits to the site kept us focused on what was important and why we were there. She came by the house almost every day and handed out hugs, baklava, chocolate chip cookies, or still-warm donuts. There was never a time when she didn't show up and start crying, saying how much her mother would have loved what we were doing. The Campbell Street house was, to Rosie, all about her mother.

Rosie's dad, Art, would also visit every day. He was a Korean War vet. (We would later renovate his house for season seven.) He brought the same photo album over each morning and told us the same story of his family, the house, and the neighborhood from beginning to end. This kept us grounded, too.

Getting the roof on was where I really learned about all that needs to be done to correctly repair burned structures. First we had to decide which rafters and wood we could keep. We then cut out the charred parts and "sistered" in new sections alongside the old. We stripped the charred sections, then primed and sealed them. It was a lot of

Lucy peeking out (top). Celebrating our progress (bottom).

The upstairs bedroom was a disaster before (left) and turned into a boy's room after (right).

work that would be hidden from view, but if we hadn't done it, the burned smell would have been in the house forever.

When the roof was finally finished, I felt incredibly relieved. It was almost July, but with the interior protected, I could get to work on everything that needed to be done inside the house. As I inspected the roof from the backyard, a neighbor came by to see how we were doing on the house. He and I started talking about the neighborhood and about Rosie, and he said, "You should have Rosie show you her gun sometime."

Her gun? "You're kidding, right?" Rosie was like the neighborhood's Aunt Bee. Everyone loved her and you couldn't be around her for fifteen seconds without getting one of her hugs. It didn't seem possible that she would be carrying a gun. So when she came by that day, I couldn't help but ask her, "Rosie, are you packing a gun?" Sure enough, she pulled up her jacket to reveal one.

"Yeah, of course. I'm a federal law enforcement officer."

"A federal agent?"

"No, *a federal law enforcement officer*," she told me.

Here I am, the person who always says, "Don't you dare judge a book by its cover," and I had completely done that with Rosie. Just because she came by every day, was emotional about the house, and brought us home-baked treats, I couldn't imagine she was in law enforcement. One more lesson the house on Campbell Street taught me: Don't be trapped by your own assumptions.

That was the way it went with the Campbell Street house. Despite all the challenges, it taught me a lot. At that moment in my life, as I threw myself into everything that needed to be done to rebuild a charred wreck, it felt like parts of my life had burned. The reality of the battle I was in for in Minneapolis was just starting to hit home. Pro-development forces in local government were looking to make me a villain. Developers were pushing back against my efforts, and the local media was taking every opportunity to criticize my work in Minneapolis. The developers would eventually gather

This bedroom looked like something out of a horror film before (left) and became a guest room after (right).

friends in Minneapolis City Hall and really come after me. That summer, I could already read the writing on the wall.

My passion for what I was doing in life, for the buildings I rehabbed and the people around me, had been flagging. But Campbell Street reignited that passion.

I knew that with a house that is half burned, you can either tear it all down or you can say, "Hey, I've got this good half left, and man, how about those plaster medallions?" I always take an optimistic approach on my houses, so that's what I was doing with my life. It wasn't "What's missing?" It was "What do I have? Let's build on that."

In any case, the Campbell Street house didn't leave me a lot of room to think about what was going on in the rest of my life. It brought a challenge a day. I lost so much time with bad weather that I just had to keep on going forward, making as much progress as possible every day on whatever part of the house I could. I was still scrambling to find the rest of my trades. My friend

Me and Ann Baxter.

The downstairs bathroom was destroyed (left). The rooms have to be spotless before we shoot "afters" (center). I noticed that the sink legs were upside down while checking my shot (right).

Kelly would get on the phone each morning, calling companies out of the Yellow Pages, off Craigslist, and anywhere else. By the afternoon, she would have made forty or fifty calls, with not one yes to show for her effort. So I did whatever I could—including getting up on scaffolding and lying on my back hour after hour fixing and painting plasterwork—to keep moving the house toward the finish line.

One day, Ann Baxter showed up and introduced herself and said, "I'm here to do your stained glass windows." I looked up at her, exhausted, and said, "I don't have a budget for that." She smiled and said, "I'm here to do your windows, Nicole, and I figured that." Ann's love for history and Detroit brought her to me. Throughout the years, Ann and her husband David's love and support have carried me through many of my projects, and at Campbell Street, Ann's appearance gave me a jump-start.

And the road was predictably bumpy. When you're restoring old houses, you have to be ready for scary surprises. One day I was in the back under a blisteringly hot sun, covered in sweat and dust, working on the small flat roof off the back office space. I was trying to remove it so I could get the new roof on and get started on the inside. Only after I'd peeled off most of the roof did I realize that nobody had ever installed a substructure. There were just layers of tarpaper tacked over the rafters. One wrong step and I would have fallen right through it.

Even worse, as I was tearing off the shingles and throwing them to the ground, one of them hit the wires going into the main electrical head for the house. Before modern codes, electrical wires were unsheathed, with no protective covering. I watched as the asphalt tile hit both lines at once, causing an arc that started a blue flame traveling up the lines, into the electrical head, and into the house. I jumped down and sprinted inside, shouting, "Everyone out! Everyone out!" Thank goodness it was a false alarm. I narrowly missed burning the house down once and for all.

Working on the bathroom with Logan (left). All hands on deck: Jose sewing on the sidewalk (right).

There were lots of other fun surprises as well. When we stripped out the still-wet wall insulation, we discovered an ant infestation. As if that weren't bad enough, they turned out to be flying ants. There was never a dull moment on the Campbell Street project.

But piece by piece, the house began to take shape. And just as I was seeing the beauty and personality in it come back to life, I also was falling in love with the neighborhood. It was like nothing I had ever seen, and certainly like nothing I had ever experienced in Minneapolis. It was like the Wild, Wild West. Feral dogs ran around looking for scraps. Guys held drag races: Starting at 9 P.M., they'd drive their cars eighty miles an hour down the empty streets. At dinnertime every night a couple of kids would steer a supercharged go-kart around the block, skidding into the turns. I walked out into the street one time and they thought I was

The Campbell Street house yard before (top) resembled a jungle. We took a machete to it to clear it for the backyard (bottom).

going to yell at them. Instead, I said, "Let me drive that thing." If you're going to be in a neighborhood like Campbell Street, you have to be part of the neighborhood.

The people up and down the street had seen a city government not only give up on the local community, but also actively rob them of their

Gramps and Ethan.

tax dollars. They didn't trust outsiders. You can go into an area like that trying to be the missionary and martyr, or you can go in there and be like a neighbor. Embrace the people, show them what you're doing, and include them. That's a part of all the houses I rehab, a part that usually doesn't make it on camera. Most of the people on Campbell Street didn't know who I was. They had never seen *Rehab Addict*. They saw the cameras and the bulldozers and the work trucks and the tiny blond chick, and they wanted to know what was going on.

So I told them. "We're rebuilding." Everyone working on the house became part of the neighborhood. And the best part of the neighborhood was its kids. There were a lot of them, as young as eight and as old as twenty. Joey and Logan. Ali and Zeke. These guys came by the work site almost every day. Jose and I became surrogate parents to all these kids. I would mother them, asking them, "Are you hungry?" "Did you guys eat lunch today?" "Did you get enough sleep?" and the dreaded question, "Have you been smoking?" While Jose, on the other hand, was the person they went to when they got in trouble with me.

The kids would always say they wanted to work, but usually, kids being kids, they would paint for forty-five minutes and then want to be paid. I'd say, "What? Put in seventeen hours like we are and then we can talk payment." We taught Logan, a small, stocky nine-year-old with a sweet round face and mile-a-minute chatter, how to mow the lawn (after we bought machetes and hacked down the backyard overgrowth that had reached epic proportions). He ended up mowing lawns all summer and making a tidy sum.

For the few hours we left the job site each day, we put our trust in the neighborhood. We didn't have security guards or even security fencing. Nothing was stopping somebody from going into the house and taking tools, equipment, supplies, and materials or vandalizing it.

The scorching weather of August came in and the house still wasn't finished. My grandparents stopped by for a visit; my Gramps refused to go inside, while my Gram was super excited and had to check out every last bit of the house. As much as I had hoped to have the house finished as we headed back to Minneapolis at the end of August, there were a thousand and one details that still needed to be finished. This was the start of my learning how to manage projects from afar; I was in Minneapolis during the week and in Detroit on the weekends, leaving Jose to hold down the Campbell Street project while I was away.

One weekend, a tremendous storm tore through the area and brought down a large oak tree at the curb in front of the house. I called Justin all excited and said, "Justin, we should carve the tree." And again with his signature noise, he said, "Nicole there's a lot more to tree carving than your hundred pounds wielding a chain saw. Why don't you do a little research and get back to me?" So, while waiting for a flight at the airport, I went

Scott Kuefler turned a tree stump into a beautiful piece of art.

Ethan and me home in Minneapolis for his homecoming before heading back to Detroit to finish the house.

online and searched "tree carving" and found the website of chain-saw artist Scott Kuefler. A week later, Scott called me and confessed, "I had no idea who you were, and I'm super busy, but when I mentioned you to my wife, she said, 'You're going to go carve this tree.' So when do you want to do this?"

When I saw Scott show up with not just one chain saw but a trailer-load of chain saws, I felt pretty silly for having thought I could've carved the tree myself. Now when people come to check out the Campbell Street house, the first thing they do is take a picture of that tree carving.

We were closing in on the finish line, and as always, I was obsessed with staging the home, raiding every retail shop, estate sale, Craigslist ad, and garbage pile to make it work. At one point, I even had Jose out on the curb taking turns sewing curtains with my mom. (Oh, did I forget to mention that Jose also knows how to sew? One more reason never to judge a book by its cover.)

While I was working away on staging the inside, the landscaping had been transformed. That mud pit had become a wonderful green side yard with a cute picket fence around it, and Logan and his classmates had helped me create a community garden. Thanks to the efforts of dozens of volunteers and Rosie and her late-night appearances to paint the baseboards in the back bedroom or to just clean up, the punch list was finally nearing completion.

The open house was a testament to all their efforts, and it was a huge success. It was my second charity open house and my first in Detroit. The

The Campbell Street open house attracted hundreds of supporters and raised money for my friend Brian.

line was insane. And who was standing by my side? Chad. Somewhere in those ashes, I had rebuilt not only that house, but also our relationship. The money raised during the open house was in honor of Brian Thomas and to help offset costs for his cancer treatments. I've known Brian most of my life—raising money for him was the perfect end to a very challenging project.

I still own the Campbell Street house, and I go back there often. People always think I'm kidding when I say I mow my lawns and weed my flower beds, until they drive by to see one of my projects and there I am covered in dirt. With Campbell Street, I go back not only for maintenance, but because of my Campbell Street kids. When I drive down the street, I have to slow to five miles an hour because there are kids everywhere. To them, I'm not "as seen on TV" Nicole. I'm Nicole the mom. The little ones wave and smile and the older ones look worried as they stand up straight and hide their cigarettes. I love that they look at me as someone they can count on. It makes me feel like a million bucks. When you're a mom, you're a mom. It doesn't matter that they're not my biological children; I consider them my own and apparently they feel the same way, as I get phone calls, pleading, "Mom, I need shoes." "Mom, I need money." I love every minute of it. I have hopes and dreams for them just like I do for my own children.

The Campbell Street project is one of the houses that best defines my work. I feel like it was pure passion that resurrected that house from the ashes of a fire. After Campbell Street, when somebody tells me something can't be done, I'm like, "Really? Have you seen my Campbell Street house? Give me a break." I planted my flag in Detroit, and proved that passion means ashes aren't necessarily an end; they also can be a beginning.

# Chapter 7

# LIVE *YOUR* NORMAL, BECAUSE THERE IS NO "NORMAL"

## GRAND BOULEVARD HOUSE AND AKRON HOUSE

Out of the ashes of the Campbell Street project came the greatest profesional success I had ever seen: The show was a hit on prime-time HGTV, and overnight I lost the ability to walk around unrecognized. Everywhere I went, people would shout, "Nicole, we love the [fill-in-the-blank] house."

Returning to Minneapolis, I knew that after I wrapped my remaining projects there, including the Summit mansion, I was done. Detroit was where I wanted to be. I was sitting on the sidelines of Ethan's soccer game in the fall when a realtor sent me the listing for a 1904 cottage on a lake in Michigan. It looked fabulous, but it also looked like a lot of work. I simply said, "Keep me posted." A few months later, Ethan and I went to Detroit for

My dining room with painted murals circa 1904.

the holidays, and I decided to take a peek. The cottage was enchanting, even without heat and covered with snow. I still hesitated to buy it as it meant giving up some of that cold, hard cash that now made up the nest egg I was so proud of. But all this changed after I got a call from Leif: The pipes had burst in my house in Minneapolis. So much for taking time off; I was on the next plane there.

When I got to Minneapolis, what I found was a homeowner's worst nightmare: Everything was frozen. This wasn't a "project"—this was my home, my sanctuary, the safe place for Ethan, Max, and our latest rescue dog, Lucy. I cried my eyes out and thought of all the work that I had put into it. The house was ruined, but as I walked through the dining room and noticed that my beloved original murals had somehow escaped destruction, I caught my breath and told myself, This isn't the end of the world. After spending the past few years watching so many people suffer through *real* problems, I knew this was fixable. I was fine, Ethan was fine; we just had one big mess on our hands. I called my crew and decided that if I was going to be working, I might as well be filming. I stayed in the house, with no heat, swaddled in a sleeping bag in front of the roaring fire with the two dogs. I was determined to get the house finished by the time Ethan arrived home, because if there's one thing I knew for certain, he was not going to be happy to go through any more construction (in fact, I didn't even tell him the flood had happened because I had just bragged at Christmas dinner that we were finally living in a construction-free zone for the first time since Ethan was born). The house was repaired, I got an episode out of it, and I made the decision to move ahead with buying the cottage.

The rest of the winter, I filmed at Summit and by summer, we were off to the cottage. Most people would have just demolished the cottage and built a bigger, gaudy home. After all, it was prime lakefront property. I figured I could kill two birds with one stone by saving the house while creating a vacation spot for the family. It only made sense that I should renovate it on camera for the next season of *Rehab Addict*. Of course, in life, what makes sense isn't always what happens.

I was completely unrealistic about the actual rehab process. I expected to be able to blow into this small town in Michigan, get the work done, and be out in a heartbeat. But as soon as I tried to get going, reality sank in. Normally, I can walk into a city building department and have a permit in an hour. But my first visit to the small-town building department was an education. The woman behind the counter told me, with a big smile, "Well, it might be three or four weeks before you get your permit." I was on a tight schedule. I wanted to be finished before the summer was over because I had to be back in Minneapolis to take Ethan to school and get back to our normal routine. Three weeks waiting for building permits was just not going to cut it.

The town was suburban bliss for everyone else, but it was quickly making me claustrophobic. Even though I grew up on seventy acres, I was a city girl. After one torturous morning realizing that I was officially at a standstill, I called the people I knew in Detroit mayor Mike Duggan's office and said I wanted to meet right away.

Two hours later, I was with the mayor's staff and representatives from the Detroit Land Bank, the organization that administers the sale of the abandoned properties in the city. They sell the homes with the stipulation that any buyer has to make the home habitable in a predetermined time frame.

They had just developed an app that let you bid on houses in real time right from your phone. One of the organization's representatives installed the app on my phone. She showed me how it worked. "Look, you can bid right now."

It was a shrewd move. Anyone who knows me knows I am intensely competitive and wasn't going to lose a bidding war if I got into one. As we sat and discussed all the different opportunities, I played around with the app. The staff pointed out an impressive 1913 Tudor that was up for auction. It was on East Grand Boulevard and had hints of Minnehaha, big with spectacular style and flair. Some women—what I used to think of as "normal" women—color their hair when they need a change. Some get a manicure, or buy new clothes. I buy a house.

All of a sudden I was in a bidding war with an investor who I would later find out had been buying up beautiful old houses and converting them into commercial buildings. I looked at his counterbid on my phone. Okay, I thought, it's on. As we bid back and forth, I said good-bye to everyone and decided to head over and check out the house. The auctions wrap at 5:30 P.M. every day, unless there is a bidding war. It was closing in on the final bid when I pulled into the driveway and thought, Uh-oh, it's in really bad shape. I saw what I knew was the ultimate budget killer: a seen-better-days Spanish tile roof. Just as the words "Oh, shit" left my mouth, my phone dinged. It said, "Congratulations, you

My winning bid.

placed the winning bid!" Be careful what you wish for.

The Grand Boulevard house was right in the middle of nursing home alley, a sleepy corner of the city. What was once a very prestigious area had been left behind. Odd breezeways connected huge mansions in the area, essentially taking two properties and making them one. For whatever reason, they were all turned into convalescent homes. It might sound

The Grand Boulevard house exterior.

dreamy to spend your final years in a beautiful old mansion, but sadly, these houses were anything but the things that dreams are made of. They looked sad and distorted with the strange bridges between them. The house I had just won at auction had not been spared; it had been used as a boardinghouse, then a halfway house, and was eventually just abandoned. It was a mix of good and bad. Beautiful white oak floors were a plus, and the holes in the roof were a minus. The plumbing and electrical systems were going to take a lot of work. It was the poster child for money pits, and I didn't care. I felt alive in the city.

While I waited for things to get rolling on the cottage, we got started on Grand. I had taken on a monster, but I loved it. The house had multiple fireplaces, each of which needed work. I wanted to create a master bedroom suite and a cool basement family room. And the roof—oh, that roof. Red clay tile roofs are gorgeous and distinctive. But when they need fixing, they are expensive. I could have trashed the whole thing for a less-expensive shingle

189

The Grand Boulevard dining room, before (top) and after (bottom) renovations.

roof, but that wouldn't have been true to the house. Instead, I found the original tile manufacturer, Ludowici Roof Tile, and ordered replacement tiles to match the existing roof. I'd end up sinking more than fifty thousand dollars into that roof; everyone would ooh and aah over it.

The house-building was on track, but Ethan was miserable. His dad was supposed to take him for the summer. Instead, he let us know at the last minute that a work issue had come up and he wasn't going to be able to. Ethan had spent most of the summer with me. We were together every single day. While I loved it, Ethan liked having the guy time with his dad, and I had to work. My job sites may have been intriguing for an eight-year-old, but they weren't exactly a sixteen-year-old's dream. And what happens in these situations, with most single parents I know, is that the child gets angry at the parent who let them down and takes it out on the one they're with. I couldn't blame E. He eventually spent a few days with his dad, but only after putting me through the wringer for even just breathing. I'll tell you one thing: As a parent, you can never assume that you have this "parenting" thing down pat. The moment you do, you fall flat on your face.

As I learned the hard way, you just have to smile and get through it. In August, with things cranking away on Grand, we started a project that I had originally begun planning the previous March, and most important, one that Ethan was all for.

I was sitting in the drop-off line at Ethan's school one morning when my agent called and said, "LeBron James's office wants to speak with you." Even if you aren't a sports person, the mom of a teenage son can't not know who LeBron James is. I repeated his name aloud. Ethan lit up. "Mom! Whatever it is, yes!" He jumped out of the car, but not without the much-dreaded kiss on the head from me. (I was fully aware that I had limited chances to kiss this precious boy on the head, and I took full advantage.) Teenage years are painful for moms like

The bathroom, before (top) and after (bottom).

me; watching your best buddy pull away while he tries to find independence is without a doubt one of the biggest challenges of parenting. If getting a call from LeBron James made Ethan happy, I was going to follow up.

LeBron James is one of the most recognizable sports celebrities in the world, and perhaps one of the most recognizable faces, period. He grew up in Akron, Ohio, which is very similar to Detroit. His life could have gone in a million different directions, but LeBron ended up a superstar. What I didn't know about him, and what most people still don't know, is that he committed at a young age to giving back. I don't mean small gestures either, but giving back in the form of gifting millions of dollars to help kids growing up in the same challenging circumstances he faced.

I learned that the LeBron James Family Foundation wanted to provide a deserving student with a house renovation as a reward for good grades and school attendance. As I've learned throughout my years of doing what I do, we tend to take for granted having a roof over our heads. What I found out in Akron was what I had firsthand knowledge of in Detroit: A lot of kids didn't have roofs over their heads that weren't caving in or leaking. How does a child concentrate on schoolwork when their house is hazardous to live in? The foundation asked if I would assist them with a renovation. After I picked Ethan up later that day, I told him the details. I still hadn't made any promises, but Ethan repeated, "Mom, say yes."

Ethan and me in Akron.

The next month, Ethan and I flew to Cleveland to meet LeBron's team. The biggest hurdle was that they wanted to do a whole-house renovation. I simply didn't have time for that. Ethan would be in school until June, and I couldn't take that much time off filming. Sitting there, Ethan looked at me and said, "Film it."

"We can't be here that long," I told him.

I added in jest, "If we could do it in a week, it's doable."

The foundation's executive director, Michele Campbell, lit up and said, "We can pull together all the trades." We discussed the logistics, the ideas flying around. By the time we left dinner—Ethan with an autographed shoe the size of my arm, and me with a whole new idea to pitch to the network—we all felt pretty confident. I pitched the idea, and the network agreed to four episodes. It was a big house; I knew we could get six, so I set my goal at that.

That summer, after months of long-distance planning, a few quick trips to Akron to walk through the property, and countless conference calls, Ethan, my dad, my dog Lucy, and I arrived in Akron to begin the project. The beauty of it was that Michele had kept her word. She had everything covered, from landscaping to plumbing, and they were using LeBron's personal builder, Jack Plas, as the general contractor. Jack had a legal pad and pen in hand when I met him. I thought, This is going to be just fine. At the time, LeBron played for the Miami Heat. Which, pun intended, he took a lot of heat for.

The renovation was part of a multiday celebration that would be held to announce something the public wouldn't know until the very last minute: LeBron was moving his growing family back to Akron so that he could play for Cleveland. Knowing all this, we had to work around LeBron's training schedule, so we had to start filming right away. Shortly after we arrived, LeBron came out of the house and said hi to Ethan first. Ethan broke into the biggest smile. Does Ethan play basketball? No. Does Ethan dress head-to-toe in LeBron-wear, and have posters of LeBron on his walls? No. But he was still in awe, and first impressions are everything. When you are famous, people love to assume and make judgments about you. Seeing how kind this man was with my son warmed my heart. We went into the house to meet the family we would be helping, and they were delightful. They had two autistic sons, which made me so thankful that Sarah and her son were en route. Sarah is like a punk-rock den mother. She's a pretty, spunky woman, with hip spiky hair, tattoos, and a broad, warm smile, and her daughter, Jane, is autistic. In addition to being my right-hand woman, Sarah would be taking on the design of the boys' rooms.

Although the first bit of filming went great, the next day we were starting actual construction. LeBron showed up with a huge entourage, including PR people, management, and just about anyone else with two cents to throw into the mix. There were all kinds of people speaking for him, which caused no end of chaos. It quickly became apparent that if I had to go through seven layers of people just to tell LeBron to hammer that nail over there, the whole thing wasn't going to work. So I took him aside and said, "You have to trust me. If we have to work like this, we aren't going to be able to finish. And with all this 'direction,' you're going to look pompous and stiff on camera. I want to give people the chance to see the real LeBron, the guy I see. You're a cool guy. Let me show that on camera."

Shooting with LeBron.

LeBron said, "All right, Nicole," and we kicked out everyone except a few people and got to work. I'm five foot three, and LeBron might as well be double that. One of the challenges of filming with someone that much taller is that I literally have to look up to speak to them. The short jokes came in packs of ten. I shot a lot of scenes standing a couple of stairs above LeBron while he was in the living room, simply to ease my neck. What I loved is that as soon as he was comfortable on camera, he went with the flow. The house was complete pandemonium, and we truly had to stick to our one-week deadline. That meant we were working on the home 24/7.

LeBron came and went around his training schedule. I just pretty much stayed put, escaping occasionally to walk Lucy or to sneak back to the hotel pool to meet up with Ethan. One day I arrived and he was sitting with Sarah's son and a group of people. He said, "Mom, come here." I walked over and he introduced me to the group and said, "They love the show. I invited them to come tour the project."

LeBron and Ethan with those megawatt smiles.

This son of mine, a teenager in full bloom, was giving me a run for my money. He had cursed the day I was born that very morning. But he was showing me that sometimes in parenting land you just have to trust yourself. My son had been gracious and engaged with this group, who had recognized his dark hair and handsome face from TV. Instead of blowing them off, he had gone above and beyond. The next day, he showed up and said, "Mom, the group from the pool is here. I'm taking them through the house."

LeBron himself became one of my crew. People would ask him, "What are you working on?" He would reply, "Whatever Nicole tells me to." LeBron could buy and sell me all day long, but I took a bit of pride in knowing he left any ego at the front porch. He went from a world where everyone said,

Giving LeBron pointers.

"Yes, LeBron," to humbly admitting this was my area of expertise. He even let me teach him how to drive a backhoe.

Everyone has since asked me, "Did LeBron really work on that house?" Yeah, he did, but not in work boots. Due to contractual obligations with Nike, the man wears Nikes every day. Sounds very comfortable, but it's not so practical in the world of demolition. We were upstairs working in the bathroom, and LeBron was helping me rip out the tub. He stepped back and all I heard was *pssshhhhh*. LeBron's staff stopped breathing for a moment. The king of basketball had stepped on a nail. And this was the sound of his Nike Air popping. I took a look and reassured everyone that his foot was safe, but his shoes were trashed. LeBron didn't miss a beat. "Nicole . . ."

I said, "Yeah?"

"You owe me a new pair of shoes."

Moments like that are my favorites. That's been the magic in my show since day one. Real moments. The tile in that bathroom was great, but it's the human story—LeBron James, about to make the comeback of his career, almost wiped out by a nail while renovating with me. Although it's quite funny to me, I'm pretty sure that moment shortened the life spans of his staff.

That house renovation was filled with joy from beginning to end. Sarah and I worked side by side, making sure that the house was just right for this great family. Her ideas for the boys' rooms were spot on, and watching those two kids jump up in delight at everything she picked made me realize how incredible my friends are. In addition to Sarah, Lauren was on-site and documented every bit with her camera and provided the best gift ever—candid family photos. I am blessed to have surrounded myself with people whose hearts grow bigger every day, and who help me make dreams come true for others.

Another part of the fun for me, though, had to be getting to know LeBron's mother, Gloria. Early on, people kept saying, "Mrs. James wants to work with you, Nicole. She's a huge fan." I heard "Mrs. James" so many times that I expected a little old lady to drive up in her boring four-door sedan, barely able to see over the dash. But then one day this beautiful Porsche came screeching up and Gloria, aka "Mrs. James," jumped out.

She said, "Hello Nicole!" and gave me a big hug that caught me by surprise. "Where is that Ethan? I want to see Ethan right now." Then she said, "Never mind. I know what that boy looks like. I'm going to go find him myself." That was Gloria. Full of spunk and fun, and an incredible spirit. She worked side by side with us. Gloria and my dad took control of the landscaping. Trust me when I say they were a force to

Ethan took Jack's caution tape to another level, wrapping the Bobcat.

With LeBron and his crew, we renovated the entire house in one week!

be reckoned with. LeBron's wife, Savannah, would show up with the boys to check out the house. She was so very pregnant and I remember looking at her, thinking wistfully, How has it been so long since I had a little baby?

Every day, Ethan would gather with LeBron's kids and the kids who lived in the house, and they'd get started somewhere working like the rest of us. Ethan didn't need me to prep him or guide him. He just said, "Mom, I got it." And off he'd go. There was a bittersweet tinge to that, because my skinny little boy with the million-watt smile was growing into a strong man who could do for himself. I could see that not too far down the road, he'd be ready to do his own thing, and Mom might take a backseat to whatever that was. On one of our last nights in Akron, Ethan joined me for LeBron's homecoming ceremony, where I was to address thirty thousand fans. Ethan said, "You got this, Mom." I went up onstage and tried to get the crowd going with the standard O-H-I-O chant. You shout out "O-H" and the crowd shouts back "I-O." Only when I got up there, I shouted "O." The crowd was silent. I was puzzled. What the hell had I done? What had I missed? Then the very sympathetic master of ceremonies came over and whispered "O-H." As the crowd booed, I tried to save the moment with an "O-H," but when it didn't work, I just laughed, apologized, and moved on. Ethan looked at me with a face that said, "Oh my gosh, Mom." He had a good laugh for quite a long time on that one. "Mom, you got booed! Like, big ones." Everyone in that stadium could boo me, but having that boy by my side was all I cared about. One of my favorite pictures is of the two of us that night.

When we wrapped up the house and headed home, I had a newfound love for Akron, and a story to cherish for many years to come. Even amid all the work between Grand and the Akron house, my personal drama kept burning. Chad and I had been going back and forth, trying to make it work.

For my thirty-eighth birthday, I had asked Chad if there were any plans. There weren't. I didn't say anything. I hung up the phone, called Delta, and simply asked, "Where can we go tonight?" I then booked two seats on the 10 P.M. flight to Amsterdam. Not for Chad and me; my birthday date would be Ethan. Chad was a bit shocked by the news, but he was a good sport and drove us to the airport.

During the ten hours in the air flying, I had a chance to just think. There's not much else to do on a transatlantic flight. I don't get much time at home for quiet reflection. So while Ethan watched

Filming with LeBron was more of a production than I was accustomed to (top). Sarah, Michael, me, and Ethan before my O-H disaster (bottom).

Our trip to Europe for my thirty-eighth birthday.

movies, I thought about the future. I had to accept the fact that this teenager sitting next to me wasn't my little boy anymore. He was growing up and would be moving on, and I was going into a new chapter of my life. What did I want that chapter to look like? Did I want to keep rehabbing homes? Did I want to travel the world? Did I want to concentrate on my charitable foundation?

Ethan and I had the best time in Amsterdam and Paris. It was the first time in years that I actually had time off from work. We had been filming *Rehab Addict* for almost six years straight.

When we got home, Chad had gathered a group of friends to celebrate my birthday at the place where we had our first date. He told everyone how much he loved me and pulled out all the big guns. I even got a diamond tennis bracelet. I tried to hide my disappointment—before you judge, I'm not a woman who wants tennis bracelets or status symbols. What I wanted from him wasn't a material thing. I wanted him to see the real me, cherish me, and celebrate me. I found an escape from this madness holding my friend's baby on my lap and took a picture, joking around that I'd gotten just what I wanted for my birthday—a baby. The next day, Chad and I finally decided enough was enough. The vacation had made me realize that sometimes you need to let things go. Even though we'd given it a good try, it just wasn't working. No regrets. I felt renewed and refocused. I flew to Detroit to take part in the Detroit Homecoming, a conference of expats who had left Detroit but were coming together to help renew and rebuild the city.

I mentioned to Sarah that I seemed to be putting on weight. She just shook her head. "You don't gain weight. I'd say you're pregnant." And I was. Here I had been psyching myself up to accept that I was soon going to be an empty nester. I was starting to think

At my birthday party, holding my friend's baby. I said, "Look what I got for my birthday!" not knowing I was pregnant.

about where I wanted to live, and what I wanted to do now that I would be forty with Ethan going off to college.

Chad's reaction to the news was not what I had expected and certainly not what I had hoped for. I had wanted my fabulous Mister to look at me with tears in his eyes and say what I was thinking: that this was the greatest thing we'd never asked for. But as much as I can fix almost anything I put my hands on, that relationship wasn't something I could repair. I was on my own. I did what I always do: kept going. This was not going to be a put-your-feet-up-and-relax pregnancy; it would be anything but.

I spent the fall commuting between Minneapolis and Detroit finishing up the Grand Boulevard house.

I watched October and November slip away, and suddenly we were into the hectic Christmas season. Ethan and I slipped away to London because

A quick trip to London with E (left). We visited Stonehenge (right).

I knew this would probably be our last opportunity to take a trip with just the two of us. I decided to keep the pregnancy to myself as much as possible. I didn't talk about it in my social media posts. With any filming we did on Grand at that point, Jose and Andrew, my camera crew, shot me from the shoulders up. It became a game of how to hide the belly. At one point, Jason Sanford's beautiful handmade vanity mirror became a prop, and I carried it through the house on camera to hide my belly for a walk-through. We slipped up only one time, in a scene with me talking to the dogs through a door. Of course, two die-hard fans managed to freeze that scene and went directly to my Facebook page to point it out.

I quickly deleted their comments. I wasn't trying to be deceptive; I just wanted to preserve some privacy and protect my unborn baby. When you have millions of followers on social media and on television and you're as outspoken as I am, a lot of people feel free to pass judgment on what you say and do. As a soon-to-be single mom for the second time, and juggling more work than two "normal" people should, I just didn't need to hear some of the comments I knew I'd get.

The first episodes showing Grand aired in January 2015, but that massive house was far from finished. We were running to keep the work caught up to the episode schedule. Complicating matters was a commitment I'd made to the network.

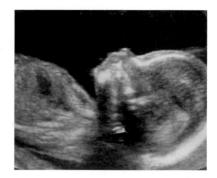

Baby on the way.

The HGTV executives had asked me to participate in a program called *Beach Flip*. It was going to be a competition show, where couples remodeled their beach houses with input from three mentors—David Bromstad, Josh Temple, and me. It wasn't really my style. I'm not a staged-show type of person. But there was this fear in me that if I turned it down, I would be thought of as someone who couldn't juggle everything. And now that I was adding to my family, I didn't want to jeopardize my relationship with the network.

The episodes were filmed in Gulf Shores, Alabama. If you look at a map, Gulf Shores is right smack on the Gulf of Mexico. I thought that at least it would be a nice getaway: white sand beaches and plenty of warm sun. Even though the show wasn't a perfect fit, I thought it could be a working vacation.

Getting to Gulf Shores from Minneapolis is no small feat. I connected through Atlanta and landed in Pensacola. That meant I found myself running, with my ever-growing belly and Lucy in tow, between gates in Atlanta's Hartsfield-Jackson Airport, trying to make my connection. But the real adventure started once I arrived in Pensacola: an hour on back roads from Pensacola to Gulf Shores. I was hoping the destination might make the journey worthwhile. I had this rosy idea that the cast would be put up in cute little beachfront bungalows with adorably cheesy seashell motifs and supercomfortable beds. No such luck. We were housed in faceless concrete-block condos with furniture that looked like it had been bought directly off the Sunday advertisements in the paper. And any illusions I had about Gulf Shores being tropically warm in February were blown to pieces as I shivered through one chilly day after another. I was pretty sure it was punishment for something really bad that I'd done in a previous life.

Restaurants in Gulf Shores, Alabama, serve two things: shrimp and shrimp. Thank goodness for Josh and David. Their bright-and-sunny personalities are not just made-for-TV; they're really genuinely sweet and upbeat guys. They were the best thing about the *Beach Flip* experience. They were good-natured champs who allowed me the honor of being their designated driver whenever we went out to take in a little local color and a bite out of a sudden forty-degree cold front.

Although *Beach Flip* involved only eight weeks of filming, it was a rough eight weeks. Ethan was still in school, and he was adamant that he would not be traveling. So while everyone else involved camped out for the duration, I would shoot the show and then catch the red-eye back to Minneapolis. It was a five-hour commute each way. Even though he was seventeen with a driver's license, just as he was opposed to coming with me, I was even more opposed to him staying on his own. By the last week of filming, I was constantly exhausted and as big as a house, and the baby was resting on my sciatic nerve. I had to drag my left leg along with me everywhere I went. I was healthy, but flying while pregnant is far from comfortable. Several times my plane was held in Atlanta due to weather. Once, the plane made it all the way to Pensacola before they decided it couldn't land, and they flew us back to Atlanta. Even for a seasoned business traveler like me, it was a nightmare. The moment that summed up the whole experience for me started out with a quiet morning walk with Lucy. All of a sudden, she pulled out of her collar and took off like the wind, racing up a parking-garage ramp. The ramp looked like Mt. Everest to me. It took me forever to get to the top. I'm sure I made quite the lovely sight, dragging my left leg behind me like a zombie and yelling, "Luuucccyyyy!" I knew full well that when Lucy took off, she came back when she was good and ready to come back. She could run for miles and miles. But at the top of that ramp, I think she just looked at this big, exhausted pregnant woman with the leg that didn't work, and she had to give up. She stopped in her tracks with a look on her face that said, "I can't do this to you, Mom. It's just cruel."

You know you're in a bad place when your scruffy rescue dog (aka Honeybadger) is taking pity on you. She calmly walked back to me, acting like I was the one who had gotten loose. I slipped her collar back on, thinking, Okay, I am so over all this. I filmed my last scene, packed up, and flew home that night.

Fortunately, I began to see the light at the end of the tunnel. The Grand Boulevard house was turning into something special. Years ear-

The *Beach Flip* team (top; I'm wearing the necklace Mina made for me). Lucy, me, and my big belly (bottom).

lier, my brother had led me to a fantastic Art Deco bar that I had bought for one thousand dollars, thinking I would install it in Summit. But given what had gone on with Chad, I now figured I'd never use it for the St. Paul mansion, so I installed it in Grand's basement lounge. It was the room's centerpiece and made the entire space look absolutely stunning.

The whole time I was pregnant, I was still making appearances, Lucy in tow to hide my growing belly.

Everything was coming together all at once. I was nearing the end of my pregnancy and ready to meet my second child in person and shower him with love. I could see that Grand was going to be finished right under the wire—just in time for the final episode and for the charity open house that would be my biggest yet. None of it might have seemed normal-looking from the outside in. But one night, walking around Grand after the workers had left, with so much completed in the beautiful house and my belly so large, I thought, Who cares about normal? And for that matter, who is "normal"? I think people get caught up wishing they were more normal, that the dramas or challenges they go through aren't what other people have to deal with. But that's not the way it really is. There is no "normal." My life isn't normal, but neither is anyone else's. Your life is only normal to you, and that's important to keep in mind when you start trotting out mental measuring sticks to compare your life to some made-up idea of what normal is.

I realized that my normal was this, being a mom—not a "single" mom, just a mom to a beautiful teenager and this baby inside of me. My new normal meant making a home in Detroit again. Fortunately, Minneapolis mayor Betsy Hodges was about to make my decision to move a whole lot easier for me.

# Chapter 8

## MAKE YOUR HOME, FRIENDS, AND FAMILY YOUR SANCTUARY

### INDIAN LAKE ROAD HOUSE
### AND RANSOM GILLIS MANSION

By the time I was completing work on the Grand Boulevard house, Ethan had made the heartbreaking decision (for me, at least) to spend his senior year of high school with his dad in California. I felt like a failure. Everyone told me I shouldn't, but I did. I was devastated. Deep down, I knew that this young man just needed a male figure more than a mommy in his life at that point, but that didn't make the sting any less harsh. With Ethan gone, Minneapolis—the city I had come to call my own—now felt foreign. And on top of all that, I felt ostracized by the new mayor, Betsy Hodges.

My problem with Mayor Hodges had started a year before, with the beautiful 122-year-old Orth house in Minneapolis. Despite the Minneapolis

I used Flat Ella to help kids identify with the lasting effect of demolition.

Heritage Preservation Commission's ruling that the house was a "historic resource" and the city council's vote to honor that ruling, a local developer and the current owner kept trying to get the house demolished to make way for a commercial development. It was just one more battle I had to fight against those who would destroy a neighborhood's identity and cart truckloads of debris to a landfill in the name of "progress" and making a buck.

Again, with old houses, once they're gone, they're gone. All the handmade craftsmanship and greatness that we can't re-create ends up in a landfill. We were losing old houses by the dozens, and in the process, losing what made Minneapolis so unique to begin with. After all, one of the things that attracted me to the city was its beautiful architecture. As in so many other cities, everything replacing the existing architecture for the sake of "density" (i.e., more housing) was what I call "disposable buildings." Nothing unique, nothing quality, nothing that would last a hundred years, and nothing anyone would marvel at if it did.

The newly elected city council, led by the developer's champion on the council, defied the previous city council's ruling and the recommendation of the Heritage Preservation Commission. The new council wasted no time voting in favor of demolishing the Orth House. People were up in arms about the reversal. In the end, we lost—the developer brought in the bulldozers and quickly turned a glorious three-story mansion into a toxic cloud of asbestos and who knows what else, filling dumpster upon dumpster with waste to build a "green" development. The greenest homes are the ones still standing. Here's why: Demolishing a house puts forty-four tons of material into a landfill. The site was soon cleared for its brand-new, slapped-together, no-personality, forty-four-unit apartment building.

I posted regularly on social media about the struggle to save the Orth House. Me being me, I wasn't going to pull any punches. In one post, I called out the councilperson supporting the developer and demolition, Lisa Bender, as someone who had said she valued neighborhoods and historic preservation, and then fought for a developer's right to tear down a wonderful old home that had stood for more than a century. The post was shared hundreds and hundreds of times over. Of course, in the nature of social media, people commented on it, some not so nicely. Hodges—mind you, an elected public leader—used her Facebook page to condemn me and demand I apologize to her city, apparently forgetting that this "reality TV star," as they referred to me, was really just a concerned taxpayer voicing her opinion. That would have been bad enough, but she decided to prove her point with references from a local activist/blogger who had been harassing me for months. He had even published my home address. As in, the place where I lived with my son and two dogs, awaiting the birth of my second child. Talk about feeling vulnerable. Her actions put my family at risk, and I could no longer ignore it. Every day, some new comment or harassment would filter through, and I was getting mail that was less than polite.

It was a horrible experience, made even worse by the fact that I had spent eight hardworking years, hundreds of thousands of dollars, and every last bit of energy I had on preserving the historical architecture of Minneapolis. Not to mention being a contributing member of the community. I never asked for high praise or the key to the city. But I certainly don't think I deserved such venom.

My beloved crew—Jose, Sarah, Andrew, and Dave—escorting me to a Detroit event.

While Mayor Hodges was busy bashing me, two states away, Detroit mayor Mike Duggan was singing my praises. At some point, the more I was in Detroit and feeling the love, the more I had to ask myself, Why are you focusing your energy on a city that doesn't want it, when there are cities that do want it? Just like with my relationships, I thought, there are other fish in the sea.

I decided to let go of Minneapolis and move the bulk of my business to Detroit. Now, don't get me wrong; I kept my house there for a few reasons: (1) Should my seventeen-year-old son make one peep that he was ready to come home, my butt would be on the next plane back, and (2) some of best friends in the entire world live in Minneapolis. Not to mention the fantastic food there. You may not know this about me, but I'm an eater. Even now, I sneak into town quite often, head down, mouth shut, and treat it like I'm having a vacation in the fabulous city I've loved for so many years.

There I was back in Michigan to have my baby, pretty much bursting at the seams. Nothing was slowing me down. I was enjoying every last minute of it. Even in ninety-degree weather and almost two weeks overdue, I felt good. Dr. Abbou, the doctor who had delivered Ethan, would also be delivering this baby. Then I went in for some tests and found out that my blood pressure was high. The doctor on call said, "I want to admit you and induce labor." I said, "No way." She got Dr. Abbou on the phone, and I could tell from her responses that he was telling her to let it go. "Nicole won't stay. She knows what she's doing." I don't really do "lying still" very well. Anxiety was getting the better of me. People are always surprised when they find out that I have issues with anxiety. They see me on TV dealing with flooded basements, contractors who don't show up, and all that good jazz. They think I let it all roll off my back. But just because you can juggle chain saws doesn't mean you don't get stressed about it. Plus, I was hungry. Unlike with my first pregnancy, I was now a woman who trusted her gut and knew her own body. My blood pressure was high due to the anxiety, and I knew what labor felt like. This wasn't it, and I wanted this baby to come when he was ready, not from being induced.

Sarah agreed to take one last photo of me before we headed to the hospital.

I called Sarah. We had agreed she would come to the hospital when I was in labor, but instead, I asked her if she would make me a late dinner. Sarah knows me well enough that she wasn't surprised that I wasn't staying in the hospital. I drove to her house. She gave me a big hug and made me a plate of buttered noodles and chicken. I wolfed it down, thanked her, and promised I would call her when I went into labor.

At eight the next morning, I woke up and knew I was having some contractions. All I could think of was that Lucy and Max had to be dropped off at the doggy spa. I wouldn't feel relaxed until the dogs were all squared away. The contractions were a bit stronger but still very far apart. Which meant that if I went to the hospital, I would just be sitting and waiting for hours as the contractions came closer together. I took a hot shower, got dressed, and packed up the dogs. I called Sarah, who said, "Girl, I'm gonna kick your ass. I'm coming to get you." I convinced her it would be easier and quicker for me to drop off the dogs myself. When I got there, I found Sarah pacing the parking lot. (The girl at the front desk said, "Nicole, when is the baby due?" I smirked, "Today.")

Sarah drove me to my doctor, who looked at me and confirmed, "Nicole, you're in labor." Was it five minutes away, or five hours? He said, "You have a while." So back to Sarah's we went. I used her sewing tape to measure my belly, took some final pregnancy photos, ate some lunch, and finally—with Sarah about ready to throw me over her shoulder—said, "Okay, we can go to the hospital, but I'm driving."

After lunch, Sarah and I met my doula at the hospital. (A doula? So many people ask me that, and I laugh. I had never even heard of such a thing the first time around. A doula is a person who supports you during labor.) And with everything going on in my life, my friends jumped in.

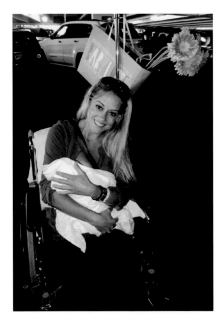

Bringing baby home.

Lauren, ever the worrywart, had interviewed and booked the doula (there was no refusing her). I pride myself on being tough and able to handle just about anything, but after eight hours of natural childbirth in a sterile hospital room, and the emotional reality sinking in of being without a partner and missing Ethan, I screamed what for me felt like words of defeat: "Give me the epidural!" A few hours later—yes, *hours*—in my epidural fog, I even asked Dr. Abbou to bring in a mirror. And then I not only felt my baby come into the world, but I watched it, after jokingly telling Dr. Abbou, "Get out

My days as a new mommy (the second time around).

of my way" (he was blocking the mirror). Looking down at my son, I was taken back to that moment some seventeen years ago when I held another little baby in my arms, Ethan, and thought, How blessed I am to be the mom to two beautiful boys.

That night, news of my son's birth had reached social media thanks to some vicious people. And I was appalled at the comments they were making. To make matters worse, a contractor whom I no longer did business with decided that he would take advantage of my vulnerable state and launched a defamatory media story about me. I was crushed. I did a news interview from my recovery room. The contractor later recanted his story, but it didn't matter. To come at me while I was giving birth was just simply a low blow.

Much to the disbelief of those closest to me, this workaholic didn't go straight from the hospital to the job site. I actually took a few days off. My body needed a break. I wasn't sleeping, but I couldn't have been happier to have this baby at my breast. And when I say "breast," I mean it. Breast-feeding is one of those things that you shouldn't really have an opinion about until you've experienced it for yourself. You go through nine long months (and then some, in my case) of carrying a baby, you go through labor, and then your body still has to adjust to feeding your baby. The best analogy I have is that it's as much fun as running in new shoes without socks across sand in hundred-degree heat. After that break-in period, it's been an indescribable bond for me and my babies.

I called my Gram every day to fill her in on the latest. She sent a crocheted blanket for the baby. My fabulous friends took turns taking care of me as I nursed the baby with Lucy by my side. If I could have chucked everything from that moment on and just focused on being a mother, I would have been incredibly happy. But once again, I didn't have the luxury of being a stay-at-home mom.

My grandparents in the 1940s (left) and in 2015 (right).

A few months earlier, two projects had come my way. The home my grandparents had built in the 1950s had been sold years ago, but by some stroke of odd luck, it was foreclosed on and I bought it. We had already started to work on it. I was directing the rehab from my very pregnant perch, but it was far from finished. At about the same time, talks of my renovating the Ransom Gillis house were in the works. It was the house James Marusich had first shown me when I came to Detroit searching for firehouses, but I had let it go to focus on Campbell Street.

I had inquired about buying it now that it was a new day in Detroit, but I was informed that the city had subsequently bundled the Ransom Gillis house with other houses and acreage in a package to be sold. The real estate developer that bought it was buying up scads of houses in Detroit, investing in the city as part of a program of revitalization. In a strange turn of events, all of a sudden, HGTV and I were in the mix to rehab and film this house

The Indian Lake Road house (original, top; during foreclosure, center; and after, bottom) was my grandparents' pride and joy, and now it's mine, too.

for TV. Even stranger, it was decided that it would be a "special series" not part of my regular episodic schedule and named *Rehab Addict: Detroit,* which would cause more confusion in future months than we ever could have imagined. I was very excited as I had thought that once Ransom Gillis was sold, I had missed the opportunity to restore it. I was told in meeting after meeting that I would have complete creative control. Given all the resources that were supposed to be available, we scheduled three weeks for the renovation. It should have been more than enough.

After all, this is what the real estate developer on this project did on a much larger scale than I had ever dreamed of. If LeBron's foundation and I could do a house in a week, clearly Ransom Gillis would be a breeze. Most important, I would just be designing the project. I could ease back into work on the Indian Lake Road house and enjoy my first few months with my baby.

If there is one place that defines who I am as a person, it's my grandparents' house on Indian Lake Road. The house was the setting for my fondest memories from childhood.

It's not the type of house anyone who has ever seen my show would expect me to tackle. It's only from the 1950s—not that old—but my grandfather built it himself. It's a sprawling, unique ranch. It also has a wonderful old red barn out back that I swore as a little girl I would get married in one day. I can't walk around that property without being seven years old again. That house is where a blond tomboy with perpetually skinned knees learned to swing a hammer, saw in a straight line (well, I'm still not very good at sawing in a straight line), and even drive a tractor.

My then eighty-nine-year-old grandfather didn't see the romance as he and my grandmother walked around the house with me. It had stood empty for quite a while. The previous owners had made some "improvements" that disguised the charm, and time had left its mark as well. I could see it was hard for him to be there. I knew deep down that the house meant a lot to him. He and my Gram had met when they were twenty years old; my Gramps was straight out of the Navy and my Gram was a salesclerk at a local clothing store. They had very little, but they had love. Over the years, they built quite the empire together. This property was simply vacant land when they used $250 they had saved up to purchase it. They built the house piece by piece—no loans, all cash. At one point, they lived in the basement as they didn't have enough money to finish the main floor. They knew every square inch of that house, and there wasn't one bit of it that didn't have their stamp on it. It wasn't their wish for it to ever leave our family, but it did, and it broke their hearts, especially knowing that it ended up looking like complete hell.

"Why would you buy this house?" he said. "I put all that time and work into this place and look how it wound up. It doesn't make sense for you to do that."

"Gramps, I grew up here. I learned how to do what I do from you. If it wasn't for watching you build and work on this house all those years, I'd be some cute elementary school teacher with two dogs, a nice white picket fence, and summers off."

"Well, what's wrong with that?" he said.

I rolled my eyes. He knew perfectly well what was wrong with that. It wasn't me.

I bought the house thinking it would bring my family together. I envisioned big family gatherings and my children making some of the same memories I'd enjoyed—running barefoot around the yard, picking cherries for lunch, swimming in the indoor pool. (Well, okay, I just sat on the edge getting my feet wet because I was not a swimmer, but the rest was there for us to share.) I also wanted to return a piece of their history to my grandparents. I wanted to show them both what they meant to me, and this house was the best way of doing that. I know better than anyone what it feels like to see something you built with your own hands disappear.

Gramps is the reason I write in concrete at all my homes (top). A picture of my Gramps's garbage removal business (bottom).

I grew up in my parents' house, but my grandparents' house was where I got to really be a kid. It was the one place where I didn't have chores, where there were always fun adventures. My parents were pretty strict, but there were no rules at my grandparents' house. My cousins and I would go outside and spend hours exploring the property, digging up large rocks to expose the salamanders hiding under them.

My grandparents did what grandparents are supposed to do—they spoiled us. If I didn't like what my grandmother made for dinner, she'd make me something else. Gramps worked hard. He was a gentleman farmer and was constantly improving one part of the property or another. Together, they built a successful garbage company, and invested in property and other businesses. He was a tough guy who worked hard and made a good living. He could be scary to people who wanted to mess with him, this short stocky guy with a gruff face and crew cut. But to us, he was just our grandpa. And we adored him.

The ranch-style house is deceptive; it looks small from the road, but it's L-shaped, and the other half of the L is actually an indoor pool. Although we had already completed a lot of the work during my pregnancy, there was still so much to do. Not to mention that there was the back apartment (the one I had retreated to all those years earlier), an old barn, and a massive pole barn. It was a lot of work, but when compared to what would occur with Ransom Gillis, it was a piece of cake.

With the Ransom Gillis house, the lunacy started almost immediately. I had assumed that we would be rehabbing the house in its original form, as a single-family dwelling. After all, that's what I'm known for: returning homes to their former glory. Imagine my surprise when I was told it needed to be designed as a fourplex.

"What?" I said. "No. I agreed to do it as a single family. A fourplex is crazy."

We went back and forth for several days, until finally the rep called me.

"Nicole, they're absolutely refusing, but they'll agree to do it as a duplex."

I was worn out. I was a few weeks postpartum. I hadn't slept, and I had been promised that this all would be so "easy," and it was turning out to be anything but. So I gave in, even though it meant I'd now be doing double the work: designing two kitchens, two dining rooms, two of everything. It was just the start of losing my "complete creative control."

At work on the Ransom Gillis mansion.

I asked to see plans for the remodel for weeks. Normally, I sketch out project plans in a day or so and have formal blueprints back from my architect within another day, so I was perplexed at what was taking so long. When I finally got the plans, I was dismayed. They called for covering up fireplaces, dropping ceilings, losing original details. Basically disguising anything that gave the building its character and turning it into two boring condos.

I don't think anyone expected me to be back at work so soon. That may have led people to assume they could just make decisions without my input. They thought wrong. I loaded up the baby, and with him sleeping nestled in his sling, I walked the house, plans in hand, redlining everything that didn't work. I soon had a meeting with the man who would come to represent to me everything that was wrong on the Ransom Gillis project. I'm not even sure what his official title was, but he was the guy calling the shots. This would be the first of many meetings where it was obvious that I'm a mom first, and if you cut into that time, be prepared to see a baby, and that baby may be on my breast.

One would think this guy and I were on the same team, and I should have been viewed as a friend rather than a foe. But it became immediately apparent that my "need" to keep the house as historic as possible had pissed him off. He showed up with an attitude, but I wanted to do this house right, so I was all business—as much as I could be with a nursing baby in my arms. As we walked through

The "glamorous" life of filming a TV show.

the house, I pointed out each feature and explained what it meant to the house and the project. He couldn't have been more unpleasant. Rather than appreciating that I was trying to meet them halfway, he was snide.

"This all sounds reasonable," he said. "What happened to the Nicole that I've heard can be so difficult?" It took everything in me not to tell him where to go, but instead I kept my mouth shut. Was I being called difficult because I'm a woman? Was it because I'm a woman who had just redlined the house plans (literally with a marker) in ten minutes and saved them more than thirty thousand dollars in construction costs (when they could have done the same thing all along)? Who knows. But what he didn't realize is that I am an expert in dealing with power-hungry men, and I wasn't going to let him push my buttons.

I would agree most of the time, however if you want unfiltered.....plz cover your tit Crack when you do a show on TV so my 8 year old can watch the glorious things you do in Detroit and elsewhere. Thank you
43 minutes ago · Edited · Like · 👍 1 · Reply

Nicole Curtis ✓
Please explain to your 8 year old that my "tit crack" is nothing bad or explicit . Perhaps explain to him that mothers nurse their children and that's what God intended breasts for,nothing else
4 minutes ago · Like

The social media post regarding those "extra pounds" (left). Filming with Andrew on the first day (right).

I would never hear him compliment a single person on that job site or say anything positive about the work we did. But all my changes were accepted. There was no reason for them not to be. My changes actually saved everyone money and time, and kept everything as historically correct as possible while building two units out of one.

We fine-tuned the remaining details, including that this was a union job. Many people didn't understand that fact, and got quite nasty with me about who was working on the project, accusing me of not being loyal to Detroit small trades. It was very simple: It wasn't my property; it wasn't my call. By the time filming commenced, I looked like I had never even had a baby. I had only a few extra pounds on, mostly on my upper half, which would crudely be commented on in a social media post after the episodes aired. The fact that I didn't look like I had just had a baby (no rock-star guru trainer here, just a combination of stress and my inability to sit still) made it all the easier to keep my new little one out of the public eye. People argued that they "deserved" to see my baby because I had shown Ethan front and center, but (1) he was twelve when we started the show and (2) had I known then what I know now, there's no way I would've included him.

On our first day of construction, I walked around and introduced myself to the crews. I explained to them that I was there to learn, and my goal was to make this house unbelievable again. They immediately let their guards down; they had apparently heard that I was a pain in the rear to work with, but when we started chatting, I found that they were just as excited as I was. Even better, they were passionate about putting their stamps on the project and making sure the iconic property was restored properly.

From there on out, every morning when I got to the site, I'd say, "Hey, how are you? How's everything going? What are you doing? That looks awesome! Why are you doing it like that? Oh, what kind of tool are you using there?" I made it clear that I wasn't critiquing; I was curious. I care what the guys who get their hands dirty building the houses think,

Checking the shot before jumping in front of the camera (top). Making Andrew stand in for me, and can you spy Jose? (bottom).

much more than I care about what the guys who handle the investments think. If the guys in the field said, "Nicole, this just isn't right," I took their word and made sure it was changed. The crew was a lot of fun, and I loved meeting their families.

The pumphouse closet, before (top). The beautiful pool bath, after (bottom), with Gramps's directions preserved.

The guys were comfortable with me. It never failed that one of them would come over to the truck as soon as I drove up and say, "Hey, Nicole, I've got something you have to see." Or, "You won't believe what we found."

At one point, I was checking out a staircase that the carpenter had just finished. "Wow, this is amazing. It's like the most amazing staircase I've ever seen. You have got to be so proud of it. I bet people tell you that all the time," I told him.

"Actually, no one's ever told me that. I just build the staircases and no one ever says anything."

That bonding was the best part of the project. So many times I thought, This is so dumb. Why wouldn't they get us all together in a room? We should problem solve this together. But the people making the decisions had problems putting their egos aside for even a moment.

Meanwhile, I was experiencing nothing but joy on the Indian Lake Road house. Every room I worked on took me back to a magical

In the pool with Ethan (top, left). The pool, during foreclosure (top, right).
The pool, newly renovated (bottom, left). In the pool with my new baby (bottom, right).

Most people gut these bathrooms (left). Unnecessary! Look at this one after renovations (right).

childhood memory. I could see my cousins and myself hiding behind the easy chair in the living room, daring one another to stroke my grandfather's buzz cut while he took a nap on the couch. The top of his hair felt so soft. When I would eventually take the dare, creeping slowly toward him, trying not to make a sound, I'd barely run my hand lightly across his hair when he would jump up with a roar to scare the bejesus out of us. He was so serious with everyone else, but he loved to be a kid with his grandkids.

Redoing the indoor pool was an entirely new experience for me. I learned a lot about how to bring a pool back to life. We repainted the walls 1950s aqua blue, and cleaned up the timbers in the cathedral ceiling. Then I redid the family room adjacent to the pool, keeping the duck-themed wood paneling and adding a midcentury bathroom where the old pool pump and filter equipment used to sit. I left one part of the wall exposed where my Gramps had written instructions for maintaining the pool equipment. I finished the floors in epoxy, which made them look like the surface of a bowling ball. The house was turning into something spectacular.

It was a dream project in so many ways, but one of the best things about working on it was that I had my grandparents to consult with, as they were in Michigan for the summer. My pet peeve with all the houses I work on is that I don't have access to the former owners or builders who might be able to tell me why something was done a certain way, which could be so

The barn on the Indian Lake Road property is so special to me.

helpful to know. On the Indian Lake Road house, I could find that out any-time I wanted. My grandparents were around all the time. I can't express enough how much fun I had hanging out with them. I knew I was blessed to have them.

Between the two projects, it became another madly hectic summer. The baby was happy and a great traveler as we shuttled between Minneapolis, where I was wrapping up my affairs, and Detroit. But the pace was wearing me out. The closer I got to finishing both houses, the more they became polar opposites of each other.

While the work on the Indian Lake Road house was moving along pretty much as I had planned, the Ransom Gillis mansion was a problem a day. In the run-up to the open house, we were working almost around the clock trying to get everything done, and getting nothing but grief. I'd end up working until two or three in the morning, trying to finish the house and accommodate the changes everybody wanted, while wearing and breast-feeding my baby. Yes, I'm a working mom, but this time around I was not going to be forced to be separated from my baby. While I was filming, the baby was on-site being cared for by one of our nannies: either my doula, Missy, or her friend, a midwife named Courtney. Having nannies might seem like an extravagance, but remember, I'm still a simple girl from the Midwest. I budget my money wisely—no fancy clothes or car—to make my life as a mommy easier.

We were downtown around the clock with the Ransom Gillis mansion, and I took refuge at all the great events the city has to offer in the summer. One of those is the Detroit Jazz Festival, and I've always been a lover of jazz. After wrapping up work one night close to ten, I ventured out with Courtney to the riverside to catch the last few sets of the festival. I was in heaven and even posted on social media how great my evening had been.

Walking back to the car, I was feeling the bliss, like when you first walk into a spa and it smells cool, clean, and crisp. That little recharging of batteries was all I needed. It reset my attitude. As we walked along, I thought, Yeah, I can do this. I can do the single-mom thing and still work like crazy and save houses. I've got this.

We were parked just a couple of blocks from Hart Plaza, where the festival was held. I had driven by the Crowne Plaza with their valet parking, but because we were late, I had decided to park on the street rather than wait in the valet line. That turned out to be a mistake.

When we returned to my truck, I saw a black SUV idling in the spot in front of us, a couple of guys sitting inside. I remember thinking it was kind of odd, but I quickly dismissed the thought.

I unlocked the car and opened the driver's side door to throw in some posters I had just bought. Leaving the door open, I went around to the rear passenger side to put the baby in the car seat. As I was strapping him in, I heard Courtney scream. I looked up and saw a man in the driver's seat. I thought, What the hell! The man obviously thought my keys would be in the ignition. I watched in shock as he rooted around for them, but thankfully they were safely tucked away in my ever-present satchel. Then next thing I knew, a woman parked down the street who was watching this all transpire screamed, "Call the police! Call the police!" I yelled, "Get out of my truck!" With that, the man reached over and grabbed my large beach bag that held

The night of the Detroit Jazz Festival.

my laptop, the rough draft of the manuscript of this book, and the cutest baby sunglasses that I would never find again, then exited my truck and jumped into the black SUV I'd seen idling in front of us.

Courtney grabbed the baby, and I ran after the disappearing SUV. I memorized the license plate and called the cops. I knew these guys would get boxed up in the downtown traffic from the jazz festival. But the 911 operator mixed up what I told her and broadcast *my* car as the one the cops should be looking for. When the cops finally got to me, they were frustrated at the screwup because they had passed the SUV on its way onto Lodge Freeway.

This is where it gets wonky. I'm not new to city life. I've had more things stolen than I can count. It comes with living in a big city. Leave a bike in the front yard and it's going to disappear. So the guy started writing a police report and I finally said, "Look, I'm gonna go home." Did I review the report? No. It was pointless. There was no chance I'd get my stuff back. It had been a long night, and I was ready for it to be over. What mattered was that everyone was safe. The report would later end up causing more problems than it was worth.

I had put up a social media post explaining what had happened a few days later. Why? Because I encourage people on a daily basis to come into the city (all cities), and I never thought to tell anyone to be cautious. Guilt was killing me. What if this happened to someone coming to see one of my houses and they didn't have the street smarts that I did? This could have been a lot worse. Had I driven our other vehicle, which has a keyless ignition, that guy who got only my bag and its contents would have been able to drive away with my truck and my beautiful baby, who was strapped into his car seat. I couldn't get the thought out of my head. In the post, I didn't mention Detroit; I kept it pretty vague. Yet the press piled on and kept calling me for comment. With each inquiry, I explained the situation and asked that they not run a story on this, but they did. And as in a wicked game of telephone, the story morphed until I was made out to be a "drama queen." I was sitting at the pool relaxing when the head of the police department called me apologizing as one of their reps had been misquoted, and the next call was my friend Rosey from Mitch Albom's team inviting me to come on his radio show and tell my side of the story. I did, but it didn't matter. People hear what they want to hear. I would continue to get ripped apart in the media for months to come.

Me with Tessa's family.

As much as I wanted to run and hide, I had to get Ransom Gillis to the finish line, which meant filming our very public open house. I don't allow photos during my open houses because I stage minimally. Props and small furniture can get knocked over or broken, or grow legs and walk away. That means I don't have lit candles, flowers, or draped towels during an open house with hundreds of people walking through. It's not safe or smart. On the day of the open house, we had a line of thousands. The money collected at the open house was going to help Tessa Prothero, the seven-year-old daughter of one of my go-to guys, Bobby Prothero. Tessa has stage 4 neuroblastoma and is one brave, tough little girl (we filmed her family's house in season seven). She stood right next to me in front of the house to welcome the visitors.

The real estate developer's PR representative showed up with a group of press photographers in tow, and walked up to the door past all the people waiting in line. I stopped them.

"Whoa, wait. Please don't take interior photos," I told them. "I'm not done with the house yet."

This PR guy looked right at me, then back at the press photographers, and said, "You can do whatever you want in this house. You don't need to listen to what she says. Take any photos you want."

It was the last straw. The press had been beating me up about everything, including how permits hadn't been pulled correctly, when I'd had nothing to do with the permits. Again, I didn't own the house. This was my hometown, where before Ransom Gillis, I could do no wrong. Suddenly, the press was all over me and my credibility was in question.

I felt so violated. To add insult to injury, I was told that before I could open the doors, I had to do a press conference. There were people staring at me from the lines, ninety-year-olds and eight-year-olds alike who had waited hours to see this house. Most important, Tessa was on the front porch with her family, and the PR reps wanted all of them to wait longer? In what some would later call an unprofessional move—but what I refer to as a single act of common human decency and courtesy—I said, "Hell, no." I went out and addressed the thousands of people who truly mattered, and I introduced the brave little girl by my side. Not one "executive" came over to Tessa and talked to her. The real estate developer had leveraged the angle that they were "sponsoring" the house, when in fact they owned it. That got the big press buzz. Meanwhile, not one news outlet ran the story on how the crew was volunteering and how we were raising money for this little girl fighting cancer. I couldn't help thinking, well . . . you can figure out what I was thinking.

Even worse, the press that did come out was critical, one article saying that the interior of the house was "underwhelming." Not a surprise, given that it wasn't staged as it normally would have been for a photo shoot. For the next few weeks, headlines like "Nicole Curtis Unhappy with Media" kept appearing. People who didn't know the truth were calling me a design hack and a diva. It hurt, but I knew the truth deep down. I was so thankful that, as at all my open houses, so many wonderful people came out to support us, waiting in line for hours with no complaints. I have no regrets about doing what I did. No one has ever called me a kiss-ass or a fake. I live life like my grandmother taught me to, looking out for the people first, protecting and helping. Overall, that open was our best ever!

But I was determined to go out on a good note with Ransom Gillis. The Thursday after the open house, I threw a big party for all the guys who had worked on the mansion and their families. They had given so much. We all had. Ransom Gillis was supposed to be a three-week project and it had turned into so much longer. All of us who actually worked on the house had paid the price. We had missed birthdays, weddings, and holidays. We had missed so much. I stated as much in a news release and again, the critics came out in droves. Isn't that what I'd signed up for? Hadn't I been paid for that? I just shook my head. I was so proud of the work that everyone had done on that house. In the end, we celebrated a lot of hard work, and it was the best time we had on the whole project. Good, bad, or indifferent, the Ransom Gillis mansion renovation was a success.

Shortly thereafter, it was time for my grandparents to fly back to Florida. I drove them out to the house and we filmed them walking through for a few minutes before we left for the airport. My Gram was so radiant, complimenting everything and sharing laughs with my crew like she always did. And Gramps finally understood why I had done that house. It was simply my gift to them. They loved it. My Gramps even wound up out front, hanging up the American flag and singing "God Bless America." Everyone had asked why I had pushed myself with everything going on in my life to get this house done so fast, but deep down I had a sinking feeling that it was now or never if I wanted them to see the house completed.

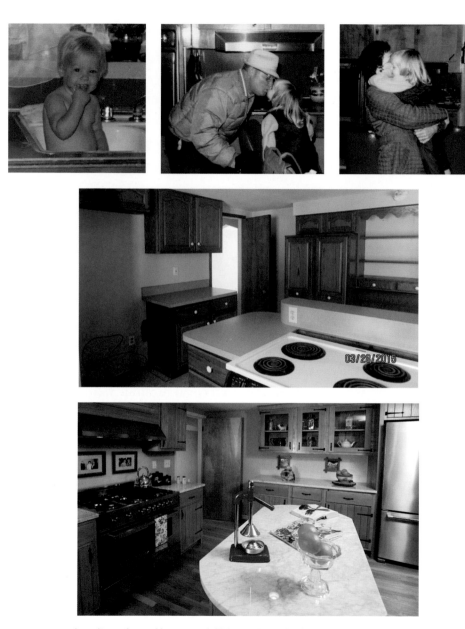

Me at the Indian Lake Road house as a child (top row). The kitchen during foreclosure (center row).
I restored the kitchen to look as I remembered it (bottom row).

My Gram and Gramps both turned ninety while we were renovating the house. The perfect gift? A 1976 Lincoln like the one they used to own. It's now parked in the garage at Indian Lake Road.

Gramps hugged me tight and said, "This is great, Pickle." After so many years, it seemed perfect that he'd use his childhood nickname for me. The story goes like this: As much as he protested his seventeen-year-old unwed daughter getting pregnant, after I was born, my Gramps would take me everywhere with him. At the bank one day a woman said, "She's so cute. What's her name?" He said, "Huh. Can't remember—we call her Pickle."

Standing there at that moment, in front of the house that really defines me, with my infant son in my arms, my grandparents by my side, it felt like I had finally come full circle in my career. After all these years of rehabbing other people's homes, resurrecting other family stories, I had rebuilt my own. It was a homecoming. So much of what happened in the summer of 2015 drove home how different a house and a home are. Ransom Gillis was just a great big house with no anchor, no person who desperately wanted it rebuilt for the stories the original structure told. For me, that left it a cold collection of lumber, metal, wires, and porcelain.

The Indian Lake Road house was, on the other hand, all about people. It *was* my grandparents. It *was* the younger me, running to find salamanders or hide in the red barn. It was rich and more than its bones.

If I've learned anything in twenty years of doing renovations, it's that the best houses are homes. Think about it. A home is where you *live*; it's your sanctuary. A house is just a structure, but a home is another member of the family.

The house is completed, and that gut feeling was, unfortunately, right on the money. My beloved Gram was hospitalized before my grandparents could come back to Michigan. I took a few months off and spent it at her bedside. I would just lie there with her, holding her hand and trying to be brave. My little boy celebrated his first birthday in her hospital room and she had a big smile, saying, "There's my baby." A few days later, my strong-willed grandmother, who swore that she just wanted to make it to her seventieth wedding anniversary, woke up for a few moments as a priest gathered us together to bless my grandparents' long marriage. Two days later, she went home to heaven with my Gramps on her right and us kids lying in her bed with her. Nothing prepares you for that. There's a lot that can be said about me, but I'm most proud when people tell me that I remind them of my Gram. She overcame so many challenges, and so have I, whether in my personal life or with the houses that I restore. Where is

Me and my beloved grandparents on their last visit to Indian Lake Road.

A happy day for this mama: me and my two boys together.

my life headed now? Who knows? But I've got my boys and my dogs, and I have the ability to handle anything that comes my way.

I've saved a lot of homes, but most certainly they have also saved me. From the first to the most recent, they have taught me respect and under-standing. As my Gram always told me, things made with love and worn with life are always better than new.

# ACKNOWLEDGMENTS

There are so many people who helped make this book possible.

To all my fans, you crazy *Rehab Addict* addicts. Thank you for the love; you rock.

To all the members of my crews and their families, including our hundreds of volunteers. Seriously, my houses would have never been finished without your time. Thank you! And to Leif, thanks for being commander in chief.

To my production teams, thank you for giving up eating and sleeping. To Andrew, Christina, Klang, Dave, and Jose, yeah, I want that shot redone.

To the police, firefighters, paramedics, and civil servants. Thank you for always coming to our rescue.

To the men and women of our armed forces and their families. The flags at my houses fly proudly in honor of your sacrifices.

To my life changers: John Kitchener, Mary Kay Reistad, and Steven Lerner. Thank you for believing in the tiny blonde who said, "I save old houses."

To my team at Flutie Management: Robert Flutie, Maryann Flutie, Shab Azma, and Danielle Iturbe. Thanks, but get me out of this Ritz!

To my book team: Judy Pray, Lia Ronnen, Sibylle Kazeroid, Zach Greenwald, Yeon Kim, Barbara Peragine, Mura Dominko, Nancy Murray, Allison McGeehon, Lauren Noess, and Chris Peterson. Thank you for doing the book "my" way.

To my wonderful friends and family who got me through all of this whether you cooked me dinner, walked the dogs, held the baby, or just took my hundreds of phone calls. Thank you.

To Ethan and Harper. I love you and you make me so very proud.

*Love—*
*Nicole*

A few of our "crew" pictures through the years.

Do you still want more?
Visit NicoleCurtis.com